THE TARA TREASURY

A PICTORIAL HISTORY OF
GONE WITH THE WIND

THE TARA TREASURY

A PICTORIAL HISTORY OF
GONE WITH THE WIND

GERALD GARDNER &
HARRIET MODELL GARDNER

ARLINGTON HOUSE PUBLISHERS
WESTPORT, CONNECTICUT

Arlington House Publishers
333 Post Road West
Westport, CT 06880

Library of Congress Cataloging in Publication Data

Gardner, Gerald C.
  The Tara treasury.

  Includes index.
  1. Gone with the wind, [Motion picture]
I. Gardner, Harriet Modell, joint author.
II. Title.
PN1997.G59G3   791.43'72   80-20385
ISBN 0-87000-482-4

First Arlington House Edition 1980
Printed in the United States of America

The production stills, advertisement and posters for the motion picture films reproduced in this volume were initially distributed for purposes of publicity and promotion by Metro-Goldwyn-Mayer, Selznick-International, RKO Radio Pictures, Columbia Pictures, Paramount Pictures, Samuel Goldwyn Productions, 20th Century-Fox, United Artists and Warner Brothers.

The photographs that appear in this book are from the files of Larry Edmunds Bookshop, Movie Star News, Cinemabilia, The Memory Shop, The Silver Screen, Yvonne Sullivan, The Collectors Book Store, Marlow's Bookshop, Book City, Culver Pictures, and UPI.

Sincere thanks is extended to Photoplay *magazine for permission to reproduce the magazine covers and magazine articles in this volume.*

Book Design by Verne Bowman

To Emanuel Modell

and Nestle Modell

without whom . . .

CONTENTS

INTRODUCTION

Gone With the Wind *has brought pleasure to everyone in the world with the possible exception of the people who made it.*

Clark Gable did not want the role. He distrusted the director, disliked costume dramas, and felt he would displease many of the book's readers.

Vivien Leigh was tormented by the role. She felt the director was too insensitive and the grueling production schedule left her wan and haggard.

Leslie Howard was opposed to the role. At forty-five, he felt he was too old for the youthful Ashley and objected to playing another watery intellectual.

Olivia de Havilland fought for the role, but felt the producer's changes were damaging the original script.

George Cukor, the director who labored on the project for two years, was fired two weeks into production.

Victor Fleming, the director who replaced him, thought the script was atrocious and was driven to a nervous collapse.

David Selznick, the producer, became a man obsessed. Sensing that this film would be the crown of his career, he drove himself and his staff unmercifully.

Yet out of all this ferment and torment emerged the most beloved motion picture of all time.

Out of enough personal conflicts to people a dozen

Harold Robbins novels came a film that has been voted the world's greatest by the National Film Institute, and that continues to be named the most popular film of all time whenever polls on the subject appear.

What accounts for the tremendous appeal of the film? Perhaps it is the energy and rebellion of its protagonist, the fiery Scarlett. Like Jane Eyre and Ibsen's Nora, Scarlett was declaring the equality of women years before such declarations were acceptable.

Perhaps it is the struggle of a society to rise from the ashes of destruction—an explanation that finds support in the film's success in post-war France, once the country had been freed of Hitler.

Or perhaps it was the genius of David Selznick, who had the time and the temerity to bring together the ideal actors, the most talented technicians, and drive them all to their greatest achievements. If genius is the ability to take infinite pains, Selznick's marathon memos and devotion to detail—in script and wardrobe and everything else under the sun—fulfill the definition.

Hollywood is like a vast amoeba seen through a microscope. Actors, directors, writers and producers continue to break up and recombine in countless new combinations. Gone With the Wind *was a combination of people who had created numerous films before fate and the judgment of David Selznick brought them together.*

This pictorial history shows the path that each of them traveled which led him to Margaret Mitchell's classic, the turmoil their union created and the aftermath of tragedy and triumph.

Perhaps the greatest magic of Gone With the Wind *is that out of this turmoil—reluctant stars, rebellious directors, a reticent novelist, and the inexorable calendar—a film emerged that had the unity and overpowering appeal to capture the minds and the imagination of millions.*

THE SEARCH FOR SCARLETT – PART I

Lombard

Harlow

Sheridan

Fontaine

Hayward

Goddard

Bankhead

Turner

Ball

Shearer

Hepburn

Young

Davis

13

There were really two searches for an actress to play Scarlett O'Hara. One was a search for publicity, the other a search for a star.

Though David Selznick had been raised on the glamour and tinsel of Hollywood, he had no illusions about discovering an unknown girl to play the most challenging role in screen history.

And so, as his emissaries fanned out across the country in search of an unknown—a girl who, in the popular mythology, would be transported from oblivion to fame—David Selznick had set himself a more realistic goal. He was determined to find his Scarlett among the constellation of established Hollywood stars.

KATHARINE HEPBURN.

Motion picture exhibitors proclaimed her box-office poison. David Selznick doubted that her sex appeal would hold Rhett Butler's interest for a period of ten years. Margaret Mitchell expressed the cautious view that she looked well in hoopskirts. The actress herself had the audacity to refuse to test for the role. And still Katharine Hepburn was very much in the running. Her friend and discoverer, director George Cukor, was bullish on Hepburn. And Selznick agreed she must be considered a possibility, observing dryly that with timeworn stars like Hepburn and Leslie Howard "we can have a lovely picture for release eight years ago."

BETTE DAVIS.

Over forty percent of the moviegoing public chose Bette Davis for the role of Scarlett, but she refused to play opposite Errol Flynn's Rhett Butler, a pairing that Bette's employers, the brothers Warner, were willing to make available to Selznick. Her bitterness at being deprived of the role was so great that she convinced Jack Warner to film a sort of fifth-carbon Gone With the Wind. And so, to Selznick's dismay, a year before the release of his landmark film, Bette Davis won an Academy Award in the title role of Jezebel, a story of a vixenish Southern belle.

NORMA SHEARER.

Though she was thirty-seven and Scarlett is sixteen when she first appears on the screen, Norma Shearer was a leading contender for the role. She was clearly past the crest of her fame, but Norma Shearer's following was too large to be ignored. Selznick floated a trial balloon. He leaked her name as a Scarlett contender to Walter Winchell. You would have thought he proposed Neville Chamberlain as Ashley Wilkes. The public outcry was horrendous. Miss Shearer's fans were apoplectic at the thought of their refined favorite portraying a Southern bitch. Undone by her gentle image, Miss Shearer withdrew her candidacy from a role that had not been offered her.

PAULETTE GODDARD.

The more he looked at her screen test, the better she looked to Selznick. But though the appeal of Scarlett O'Hara lay in her willingness to flout society's rules, the actress who played Scarlett could not afford to do so. And it appeared to many that Paulette Goddard was living with Charles Chaplin without benefit of clergy. When Selznick announced his interest in Miss Goddard as Scarlett, the women's clubs of America screamed with pain. And when Paulette Goddard was unable to produce a marriage license for Selznick's inspection, she was struck from the shortening list of Scarlett hopefuls.

15

◄ANN SHERIDAN.

Selznick had a recurring fear that his casting of the principal roles of Gone With the Wind *would be safe, secure, solid and ultimately pedestrian. So Ann Sheridan held a special appeal. She had just burst upon the scene in a string of Warner Bros. films, and Selznick liked what he saw. The producer deemed Ann Sheridan a distinct possibility, or as Sam Goldwyn would have expressed it, "a definite maybe." But soon her name slipped from the gossip columns and she was eclipsed by more prominent stars.*

MIRIAM HOPKINS.

Because she had played Becky Sharpe, a motion picture heroine who shared many characteristics with Scarlett O'Hara, Selznick felt no need to test her. He read Miss Hopkins, screened the film, and that was enough. The similarities between Thackeray's and Margaret Mitchell's heroines had not gone unnoticed by the press, and this seemingly provided Miss Hopkins with an inside track. There was an intensity to her beauty, and of course she had the added virtue of coming from the South. However, on screening Becky Sharpe, Selznick could muster little enthusiasm for the actress.

LANA TURNER. ▶

Selznick tested the pneumatic starlet who allegedly had been discovered behind a soda fountain at Schwabb's. He found her to be completely inadequate, too young and inexperienced to understand the character and complexities of Scarlett O'Hara. Whether the years brought her any greater insight into the character of complex heroines is a question beyone the province of this volume.

MARGARET MITCHELL.

The public was hungry for any scrap of gossip on the frontrunners and dark horses in the Scarlett Sweepstakes. At one point the press picked up a rumor that Scarlett would be played by none other than her creator, Margaret Mitchell. According to the newspaper story, the novelist had been observed taking acting lessons at Selznick's Culver City studio. For a woman who wanted not the remotest involvement with the film, to be cast in its lead was patently incredible. But there were evidently no limits to the credulity of the news-hungry public.

TALLULAH BANKHEAD. ▶

Like Margaret Mitchell's famous heroine, Tallulah Bankhead was a daughter of the South. Her extravagant personality had dominated many stages but failed in its transition to the screen. There was about her a frankly sexual quality that might be useful in portraying the stormy Scarlett, but Selznick found her too emphatic. Tallulah was hungry for the role of Scarlett but her tests failed to satisfy the producer. He secretly cherished the hope of persuading Tallulah to play the madam in the Atlanta brothel, but was afraid to offer her the role, fearing an explosion of her ire. He entrusted the ticklish task to a subordinate who understandably chose to ignore the assignment.

MARGARET SULLAVAN.

Like Carole Lombard, Margaret Sullavan was a client of David Selznick's brother Myron, who ultimately brought the producer Vivien Leigh. But the seeming advantage brought the actress little more than exposure. Just as Myron Selznick would negotiate as brutally with his brother as with any other producer, so David would show no fraternal favoritism in casting his films. And Margaret Sullavan got no more than cursory consideration from David Selznick.

LUCILLE BALL. ▶

Selznick invited all the studios to send over any contract starlets who might be suitable Scarletts. So one rainy afternoon a redheaded comedienne named Lucille Ball arrived at the Selznick lot. The rain-drenched actress was shown to the producer's empty office, told to wait, and had a glass of brandy thrust upon her. Selznick arrived as she was drying her hair. Miss Ball read briefly for the role and was promptly dismissed. Years later, when Lucille Ball was producing her popular TV show, she bought the Selznick studio and moved into David's old office.

JEAN ARTHUR.

At thirty-three Jean Arthur was more a woman than a girl, and her offbeat charm held no hint of the Southern belle. Still Selznick tested her for the role of Scarlett. One suspects his motive was not entirely professional. Prior to his marriage to Louis B. Mayer's daughter Irene, David Selznick was very much in love with Jean Arthur. So when he ordered her screen test, it was one of those rare occasions when Mr. Selznick's heart ruled his head.

JOAN FONTAINE.

She was twenty years old and under contract to RKO when Joan Fontaine was invited to the office of director George Cukor to read for the lead in Gone With the Wind. She had had little success at RKO and the role of Scarlett would have been a plum. But arriving at Cukor's office, Miss Fontaine learned that she was not being considered for the role of Scarlett. Selznick and Cukor felt she would be ideal as the demure Melanie. Miss Fontaine snapped that the Melanie role did not interest her. As she headed for the door she said, "Oh, you might speak to my sister Olivia."

SUSAN HAYWARD.

Selznick was wary of casting suggestions made by his wife, Irene Mayer Selznick. He relaxed his wariness when she encountered a pretty hat model named Edythe Marrener at a Manhattan fashion show. David tested the girl, and Edythe Marrener was emboldened to change her name to Susan Hayward. Unfortunately for the hat model, the test found her rather wooden and amateurish, and she promptly dropped out of contention.

CAROLE LOMBARD.

Selznick considered her fleetingly. Certainly the Gable-Lombard affair would have been immensely exploitable, just as the Leigh-Olivier romance would open a rich vein of publicity. But Selznick had trouble reconciling the zany humor of Carole Lombard with the fiery vixen that was Scarlett O'Hara.

Crawford

Young

Harlow

OTHERS.

As the days dwindled down to a precious few, and Selznick knew he must soon begin production, the producer's search for Scarlett became more desperate. The most incongruous Scarletts were considered. Their names read like a Who's Who of Hollywood, running a gamut of age, style and suitability. They included Claudette Colbert, Jean Harlow, Joan Bennett, Loretta Young, Joan Crawford, Irene Dunne and Marie Dressler.

But time was running out, and for David Selznick the hour of decision was approaching.

THE SEARCH FOR RHETT BUTLER

Colman

March

Baxter

A motion picture producer is supposed to make decisions. That is his duty and his privilege. He decides on the project, the director, the writer, the star. For David Selznick, the decision of a star for the role of Rhett Butler was taken out of his hands. The public had decided on Clark Gable.

But Gable was under exclusive contract to MGM and Selznick knew his father-in-law, Louis B. Mayer, would exact a fearful price for Gable's services. So, as precious time ticked away, Selznick thrashed about in search of another actor.

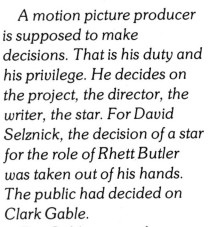

Rathbone

Cooper

Marx

Flynn

ERROL FLYNN.

The swashbuckling Flynn had the dashing good looks that the role of Rhett demanded and he was eminently available. Warner Bros. offered Flynn and Bette Davis to Selznick in a package deal for twenty-five percent of the gross and distribution rights. But in Selznick's judgment, Errol Flynn's acting abilities would be outstripped by the role of Rhett. Flynn was out of the running.

GARY COOPER.

Selznick approached Sam Goldwyn who held Cooper's contract. It seemed a felicitous arrangement, since Goldwyn's United Artists was the distributor of Selznick's films. But Goldwyn was adamant in his refusal to loan Gary Cooper to Selznick. The search for a surrogate Gable continued.

WARNER BAXTER.

Like Rhett Butler, he was a native of the South and had the South's support. But even his most ardent fans could not claim any sex appeal for Warner Baxter, and Rhett Butler exuded sex appeal from every page. The search went on.

RONALD COLMAN.

Though Gable, Cooper and Flynn were Selznick's first choices for Rhett, he carefully considered Ronald Colman. Early in the casting process, Selznick excitedly phoned Colman to read him some of Rhett's dialogue. "Ripping!" said the actor as Selznick's ardor cooled. Colman's British accent troubled the producer as much as his habit of vacillation, and the Englishman was put on a back burner.

FREDRIC MARCH.

Selznick had cast Fredric March as the fading actor in A Star Is Born and this unintended audition showed him to good advantage—a charming, adroit actor and a possible Rhett. But suddenly allegations began to appear in the public press that Fredric March was a member of the Communist Party.

BASIL RATHBONE.

Many of the readers of Margaret Mitchell's novel saw Rhett as something of a villain, and these readers lobbied for Basil Rathbone. His supporters were surprisingly numerous, considering Rathbone's menace and his British accent—but Mr. Selznick was unimpressed.

GROUCHO MARX.

Margaret Mitchell preserved her privacy with a vengeance. She refused to participate in any way in the production of Gone With the Wind. She refused to consult with Selznick on the script or write a line of dialogue for the screenplay. And she refused to be drawn out on the subject of casting. Her one suggestion related to the role of Rhett Butler. She thought Groucho Marx would be splendid in the role.

THE
CHEMISTRY
OF
OTHER
COUPLINGS

Baxter

Turner

Gable

Hepburn

Shearer   Rathbone

Leigh

March

Cooper   Goddard.

Davis.

Flynn

Marx

Ball

GABLE
FEVER

Perhaps the reason why David Selznick never managed to acquire the services of Cooper or Flynn or Colman as Rhett Butler was that he secretly suspected that no one but Gable could play the role.

Certainly this view was held by millions of Americans. Since Gable first appeared on the flickering screen, he had been galvanizing audiences with his mixture of machismo and charm.

Rumor had it that Margaret Mitchell had created the character of Rhett Butler with Clark Gable in mind. This was the most arrant nonsense. When Miss Mitchell created the character of Rhett on her battered Underwood, Clark "Billy" Gable was an unknown extra in a sea of anonymous Hollywood hopefuls.

In the years before Gone With the Wind crowned his career, Gable went through the years of struggle that seem a prerequisite of stardom. Born in Cadiz, Ohio,

to an oil driller and his delicate wife, Gable's German descent would later be kept a close secret by MGM's publicity department, especially since his family name had been anglicized from "Goebel," a name uncomfortably close to that of Hitler's propaganda chief, Dr. Joseph Goebbels.

After two years of high school, young Clark moved to Akron and joined a local theatre group. He appeared in various stock companies and landed in Hollywood in the midst of the silent era. He appeared as an extra in a few MGM films, but it was the stage that finally brought him to Hollywood's attention. His riveting performance as the doomed gangster in The Last Mile on the Los Angeles stage impressed Lionel Barrymore, who brought Gable to the attention of the Metro brass.

For a relative newcomer, Gable began traveling in some high-powered cinematic company. Within a year, the jug-eared actor

appeared with Joan Crawford in Possessed, Greta Garbo in Susan Lenox, and Norma Shearer in A Free Soul. His broadshouldered performance opposite the elegant Miss Shearer galvanized female audiences across the country.

When sound arrived in Hollywood, Gable made the transition easily. His distinctive voice captured the hearts of female audiences as much as his leering good looks.

Few of Gable's films have been cited as examples of great filmic achievement, yet Gable amassed a huge following. In films like Call of the Wild, Test Pilot, San Francisco, and Idiot's Delight, Gable continued to delight the moviegoer. He conveyed a cynical manliness that appealed to men and women alike.

It was probably beyond Gable to achieve the subtlety of a fine artist who can play many different roles. Oscar Wilde observed that people like an artist who keeps painting the same picture because they can immediately recognize his work and therefore feel like connoisseurs. In much the same way, movie audiences enjoyed seeing Gable play virtually the same role year after year.

Shy and self-conscious, Gable knew agonies on the set. His self-doubts, had they been widely known, would have damaged his box-office potential, so MGM'S publicity department had the task of hiding his uncertainties, just as Metro's creative people had the task of providing him with roles that would not tax his talents.

Gable found support for his macho image in director Victor Fleming, who would later guide him through Gone With the Wind. In his rapid rise to stardom in the early thirties, when Gable was costarred with Jean Harlow in Red Dust, director Fleming was there to present his friend as a new breed of actor, in the image of Fleming himself.

The thirties were busy for Gable. After winning an Oscar for It Happened One Night, Gable was starred in Mutiny on the Bounty, then cast opposite Rosalind Russell in China Seas, and loaned to Darryl Zanuck for Jack London's Call of the Wild.

By the time David Selznick had bought the rights to Margaret Mitchell's bestseller, he was to find that only Clark

With Claudette Colbert in It Happened One Night *(1934)*

With Greta Garbo in Susan Lenox *(1931)*

Gable could play Rhett Butler. The public would not be denied. If the motorcycle-riding, cigar-chewing, hunting, loving, fighting, daring actor was not precisely the blockade-running rogue that Margaret Mitchell had created, the public saw them as one. A long chain of films, supported by the MGM publicity mill, had done its work. Gable was Rhett and Rhett was Gable and that was that.

With William Boyd in The Painted Desert (1931)

With Marjorie Rambeau in Hell Divers (1931)

With Charles Laughton in Mutiny on the Bounty *(1935)*

GABLE AND SEX

Of all the ironies of Gone With the Wind, *perhaps the greatest is that the man who personified sex appeal to the American public, and so was the mandatory choice for the role of Rhett Butler, was profoundly uncertain of his own sexual prowess.*

In film after film, opposite a pantheon of Hollywood starlets, Gable symbolized sexual potency and the cocksure male. The message of these films was not lost on his growing public.

Gable received obscene fan mail from men and women alike, promising all sorts of erotic joy in exchange for a brief meeting. Nonetheless, Gable doubted his own sexual powers. Carole Lombard, his lover of three years and wife of two, would refer to him as "not the most terrific lay."

During his early years with touring companies, numerous matronly actresses tried to lure the young Gable to their beds. He seems to have exuded a strong appeal to older women, and the appeal must have been reciprocal: his first two wives were women considerably older than himself.

Part of Gable's doubts about his appeal to women stemmed from his self-consciousness about wearing false teeth, the result of a childhood in which orthodontics was unavailable to the struggling Gables.

To his growing public, Gable seemed to cope with women and trouble with the same cocky self-assurance, the challenging stare, the arrogant smile. Sam Goldwyn once shocked Hedda Hopper with the observation, "When Clark Gable comes on the screen you can hear his balls clanking together."

But offscreen Gable was not the confident male that the projector revealed.

Gable's first wife was Josephine Dillon, fourteen years his senior and his drama coach. When the forty-three-year-old Maria Langham, the wealthy widow of a Houston oil man, married the twenty-six-year-old Clark, she took him to Broadway and helped establish him on the stage, after which she financed the Hollywood production of the Broadway hit, The Last Mile. *Gable played the lead, and it led to a screen contract and success. The success, in turn, led to divorce.*

Gable's sex appeal continued to advance his career. An affair with Metro star Joan Crawford paved the way for a role in one of her films for the obscure contract player. Yet despite Gable's romances with a sequence of stars, he always seemed most content with the call girls from a local bordello where he could abandon the masquerade of the cocky, challenging super-male. With them he could be the simple farmboy-turned-actor and forget the fictional prowess of Clark Gable.

With Joan Crawford in Possessed *(1931)*

With Myrna Loy in Men in White *(1934)*

With Greta Garbo in Susan Lenox *(1931)*

With Mary Astor in Red Dust *(1932)*

32

With Norma Shearer in Strange Interlude (1932)

With Helen Hayes in The White Sister (1924)

With Carole Lombard in
No Man of Her Own *(1932)*

With Mamo in Mutiny on the Bounty *(1935)*

34

WHY GABLE SAID "NO"

Fearing usurious terms for Gable's services from MGM, David Selznick turned elsewhere—and no one was happier than Clark Gable to see the cup pass.

Gable had serious doubts about handling the demands of the role. He felt that the legions who adored Margaret Mitchell's bestseller had their own ideas of Rhett Butler, and so he could not fail to displease a great many people.

The dramatic requirements of the role also worried him. MGM had observed Gable's insecurities about his acting talents and had chosen for him roles that were short on sensitivity and long on action. It had handpicked directors with the same masculine propensities. But Gone With the Wind would require more than Gable had ever been asked to deliver.

To Gable's further dismay, Selznick had already chosen George Cukor as his director, a man of sensitivity who was known in Hollywood as "a woman's director." Gable

In Parnell (1937)

feared that Cukor's attention would be focused on Scarlett and Melanie, and that Rhett Butler would be left to shift for himself.

Gable's idea of a director was Victor Fleming, who had directed him in Test Pilot. Fleming was an outdoorsman with a relish for horses, fast cars and women. He was a man after Gable's own heart.

Beyond the subtleties of the character and his doubts about the director, there was one other aspect of GWTW that troubled Gable. A year before, after a string of unparalleled hits, Clark Gable had made a potboiler. The film was Parnell and it was a costume drama. As Parnell, the Irish revolutionary, Gable wore costumes that were uncomfortably similar to those of Captain Rhett Butler.

But whatever his doubts, there was a most compelling reason to play the role of Rhett when it was offered to him. And that reason was Carole Lombard.

With Carole Lombard in No Man of Her Own *(1932)*

Clark Gable had fallen in love with a madcap comedienne named Carole Lombard and their lengthy love affair was known throughout the industry.

Gable wanted his freedom from his second wife, Rhea Langham Gable, but she refused to grant it. Unknown to Gable, Louis B. Mayer, the emperor of MGM, encouraged Rhea Gable to raise her demands to an exorbitant level. The lady consequently demanded $265,000 as a divorce settlement, a terrible price to pay for love and freedom. Mayer magnanimously agreed to give Gable a $100,000 bonus for playing Rhett, a sum that would soften the pain of the hefty settlement. Gable reluctantly agreed, and the perfect actor met the perfect role.

If Gable knew of Mayer's friendship with his wife's lawyer, it may well have crossed the actor's mind that the studio head was using Gable's personal anguish to force him to accept a role he feared, in exchange for a release from a conjugal bind.

And so, from a man who would not play Rhett Butler for love or money, Clark Gable became a man who played him for precisely that—Lombard's love and Mayer's money.

Faust's business arrangements with the devil were no more demanding. But the actor's deal had its rewards. With the divorce finalized, the King was free to marry Miss Lombard, and he wasted no time in acting on the opportunity. Avoiding the extravagant nuptials that Mayer preferred for his two superstars, Gable and Lombard drove to the small town of Kingman, Arizona. Gone With the Wind was already before the camera, but Selznick graciously gave the lovers two full days for their honeymoon.

The ceremony put an end to three years of secret meetings in hotel rooms where Gable and Lombard's fears of damaging publicity drove them.

Gable could take some consolation in knowing that he was not the only one who had paid an extravagant price for the fulfillment of his needs. David Selznick had also gone riding on the tiger and returned inside.

When Selznick walked into Louis B. Mayer's office to bargain for Gable, the cards were all in his father-in-law's hands. Mayer exacted a terrible price for the star's services: MGM would put up half the film's $2,500,000 budget, plus Gable, and receive in return half the profits and full rights of distribution.

THE DE HAVILLAND CAMPAIGN

It may be that the meek shall inherit the earth, but certainly not in the area of Hollywood, California and certainly not in the circle of Hollywood actresses. A fine example of this rule of thumb may be found in the career of Olivia de Havilland who achieved her success by a dogged determination that was well concealed behind her soft brown eyes.

Working at Warner Bros. in the early thirties, Olivia found herself in what appeared at first to be an enviable position for a young starlet—she was repeatedly cast opposite a handsome newcomer named Errol Flynn.

First it was the film version of Sabatini's swashbuckling Captain Blood, *then the delicate Maid Marian to Flynn's dashing* Robin Hood.

But with the passage of time, Olivia began to see the worm in the apple. Flynn's career was skyrocketing; Olivia's was at a standstill.

Warner's was not the ideal lot for an actress. The studio's gritty, broad-shouldered films were dominated by gritty, broad-shouldered actors—Cagney, Muni, Robinson, Bogart.

Olivia's assignment was to look demure in the wake of Errol Flynn. Indeed, she proved so skillful at simulating sweet submission that she was cast as the doe-eyed darling for a whole succession of Warner's male stars. Her sweetness was enough to decay the teeth at twenty paces. It was a little much for the assertive, ambitious actress to bear.

On top of this, her contract required her to appear in all those films to which she was assigned, and this included a long string of forgettable specimens. As a contract player, Olivia was subjected to a subtle form of peonage. If she refused a role, she could be punished by immediate suspension without pay. It was a Catch-22, for Olivia found herself typecast in a specific role that had stopped her career dead in its tracks.

Loan-outs were rare at Warner Bros., and brother Jack felt it was a form of subversion second only to espionage to refuse an assignment.

That was the state of Olivia de Havilland's career when David Oliver Selznick began to cast the major roles in Gone With the Wind.

When Joan Fontaine suggested to director Cukor that he read her sister for the role of Melanie, Olivia realized that Jack Warner would be a barrier to the role. So when Cukor acted on Miss Fontaine's suggestion, Olivia kept her visit to Cukor's office a secret. And once she had read the part to Cukor's satisfaction, her trip to David Selznick's hilltop home was even more clandestine.

Cukor had chosen a scene for Olivia to read that he felt would display her ability to its best advantage. Unfortunately, it was a scene between Melanie and Scarlett, and at the secret meeting there was no one

present with whom Olivia could play the scene. Undaunted, director Cukor played Scarlett to Olivia's Melanie. Cukor gave an inspired performance as the emotional vixen, as Olivia struggled to suppress her laughter. She gave a moving performance and Selznick decided on the spot that Olivia was his Melanie.

But not quite.

Olivia, as has been noted, was under contract to Jack Warner who was unlikely to relinquish his iron grip. When Selznick approached him, the predictable answer was a deafening no. Warner's attitude was not blindly tyrannical. He feared that once the actress had tasted freedom, she would be unwilling to return to the regimen of studio assignments.

Olivia saw that though it was the limpid loveliness of Melanie that had gotten her the part, it would take the tempered steel of Scarlett to get her the release. She determined to go over the boss's head. She went to his wife.

Olivia had once met Mrs. Warner at a party and they were hardly intimates, but Mrs. Warner was a former actress and could be expected to sympathize with Olivia's plight. The two women met for tea at the Brown Derby. Pouring out her feelings to Mrs. Warner, Olivia enlisted her aid in persuading her

With Errol Flynn in Santa Fe Trail *(1941)*

With Errol Flynn in Dodge City *(1939)*

With George Brent in In This Our Life *(1942)*

husband to grant Olivia her temporary freedom.

Warner exacted a modest price for his generosity—the loan of newcomer Jimmy Stewart from Selznick for an upcoming Warner Bros. film, No Time for Comedy. But Warner did not profit from the arrangement. The price he ultimately paid in the de Havilland loan-out was more than he could have anticipated.

Warner foresaw that Olivia would be an unwilling captive of the back lot once she had tasted freedom. But he never could have dreamed that she would become the front-runner of rebellion on the Warner lot, that she would defy the studio in a landmark case that dragged Warners through the California courts and finally brought it to its knees.

"NOT ANOTHER WEAKLING"

Of the four stars of Gone With the Wind, *two would have sold their souls for the part, and two would have sold them to avoid it. Vivien Leigh used all her wiles to capture the role, as did Olivia de Havilland. Gable was never comfortable in the role and had to be dragged to it.*

Leslie Howard was even more strongly opposed to playing Ashley Wilkes, but for a different reason.

At forty-five, Leslie Howard felt he was much too old and not nearly attractive enough to play the handsome young man that Margaret Mitchell had created. He knew it would mean months of being prettified by an army of makeup men to give him the bloom of youth and the attractive sheen that the role demanded.

More basic still was the character of Ashley. He was a dreamer, an artist, an intellectual, an idealist. In short, he was one more in the long line of watery weaklings that Howard had been

In Of Human Bondage *(1934)*

In Outward Bound *(1930)*

With Conchita Montenegro in Never the Twain Shall Meet *(1931)*

In Stand-In *(1937)*

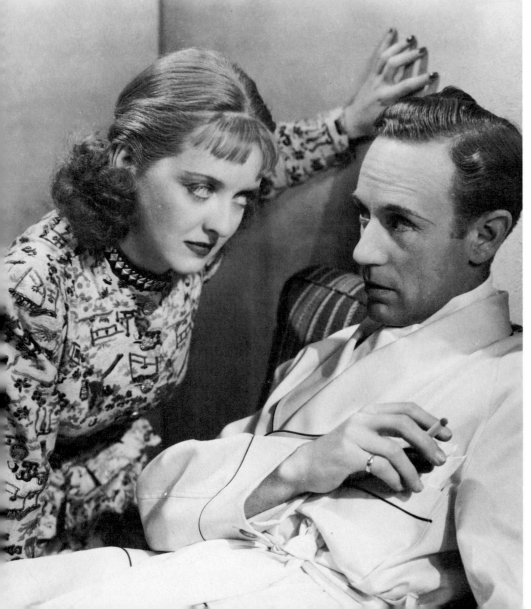

playing all his life. Like Olivia de Havilland's doe-eyed damsel in distress, Leslie Howard was hopelessly typecast as the troubled man of thought, and he had had it up to here.

Leslie Howard sought a career in acting when he returned from the front lines during the carnage of the First World War—anticipating the scene when Ashley returns from another war to the waiting arms of Melanie and the covetous glances of Scarlett.

Howard observed that there was a shortage of actors on the London stage, since the cream of British youth

With Bette Davis in
It's Love I'm After *(1937)*

was off fighting in France. He therefore sought a job in acting, and promptly found one. Surprisingly, his most successful role at the time was in Charley's Aunt.

By the late 1920s, Leslie Howard had developed his craft, and with his wife and young son, set sail for America. He received excellent notices in the Broadway drama Just Suppose and held his own with the major stars of the Broadway theatre—Alfred Lunt in Outward Bound and Katharine Cornell in The Green Hat.

Off to Hollywood in 1931, he had his first contact with the monolithic Metro-Goldwyn-Mayer, where he made three films. One of these was A Free Soul, with newcomer Clark Gable. Then, after a Broadway success in The Animal Kingdom, Howard worked for producer David Selznick in the film version of the play. Next Howard was cast in Somerset Maugham's Of Human Bondage, with an actress who would later covet the Scarlett role, Bette Davis.

By now Leslie Howard could see the pattern for which he was being chosen. In Of Human Bondage he played the weak, watery idealist that he would play again and again until the role became his by patent.

In The Scarlet Pimpernel he once again played the weak intellectual—and if the weakness was merely a cover for the audacious Pimpernel, this did not prevent America's casting agents from observing how well Howard played the weakling.

So when Robert E. Sherwood created still another idealistic intellectual in his play The Petrified Forest, it was again Leslie Howard who was summoned. A newcomer named Humphrey Bogart played the killer, Duke Mantee, and impressed Howard. So when Warners wanted Howard to star in the inevitable Hollywood version, he insisted that he would only take the part if the unknown Bogart were allowed to re-create his role in the film. Warner Bros. reluctantly agreed. Thus Bogart found a career, Warners found its most valuable star—and Leslie Howard continued to bear the cross of the watery weakling.

In 1935, Irving Thalberg, the young production chief at MGM, was engaged in a talent search to find a leading man to play opposite his wife Norma Shearer in Romeo and Juliet. The talent search was every bit as spurious as the search for Scarlett O'Hara. Thalberg knew he wanted Leslie Howard. But Howard resisted. By now he was past forty and could not picture a middle-aged actor playing the youthful Romeo. But Thalberg prevailed, and the actor's resistance to the role of Ashley Wilkes four years later would be forged in the fire of Romeo and Juliet.

Then came a great moment in Leslie Howard's screen career. Most actors, if they are fortunate, can boast of one film that commands both critical acclaim and great public acceptance. Leslie Howard had two—Gone With the Wind and Pygmalion.

An audacious young man named Gabriel Pascal had gone swimming off a Scottish beach in order to meet playwright George Bernard Shaw. The playwright had resisted all efforts to acquire the movie rights to his plays. ("The difference between us," Shaw had once told Sam Goldwyn, "is that you are interested in art and I am interested in money.") But Pascal had persuaded Shaw to let him option Pygmalion. The result was screen magic, the coruscating wit of Bernard Shaw delivered with the impeccable style of Leslie Howard as Professor Henry Higgins.

And once again Leslie Howard was cast as the intellectual.

By the time David Selznick was ready to cast the role of Ashley Wilkes in Gone With the Wind, two conditions clearly obtained—there was only one actor who could play the role, and that actor was inexorably opposed to playing the part.

THE SEDUCTION OF LESLIE HOWARD

David Selznick had squandered so much time on the fraudulent talent search for an unknown actress to play Scarlett O'Hara that he left himself no time for what he really needed — a talent search for an actor to play Ashley Wilkes.

His need for an Ashley was greater than his need for a Scarlett. There were a few actresses who could have played Scarlett creditably, but there was only one Leslie Howard. And that man hated the role. He had been playing it all his life.

As the starting date neared, Selznick was frightened at the impasse. True, Irene Selznick had observed that Ray Milland was attractively weak, but Selznick thought Milland's accent was wrong. True, Melvyn Douglas was a fine, sensitive actor, but his beefy appearance was not right for the introspective Ashley. True, Lew Ayres had his supporters, but Selznick was not among them. Nor did he respond to the screen test

of Jeffrey Lynn. There was really no one but the actor who had lit up the screen in The Petrified Forest and Pygmalion. But unfortunately, Mr. Howard wasn't having any.

Approached by Selznick, Howard flatly refused even to look at the Margaret Mitchell novel. Reluctantly he scanned a few scenes that playwright Sidney Howard had written for the screenplay. The other Mr. Howard was unmoved.

The irresistible force had met the immovable object. And it was here that Selznick proved his mettle as a producer. Assembling a cast is more than making a list; the producer's job is never that simple. In the case of Leslie Howard it called for finding the right button to push—the right area of temptation. With Gable it had been money for an embittered wife. With Howard money would not do.

Selznick knew that Leslie Howard was a man with

literary gifts. He knew that at heart Leslie Howard was more anxious for employment on the other side of the camera—as producer or director or writer. Fortunately for David Selznick, this hunger for the dark side of the camera was the instrument that would bring Leslie Howard to heel.

Selznick's proposal to Howard was as shrewd as it was effective. It was a package deal: Leslie Howard would play the idealistic Ashley Wilkes, and in addition, in Selznick's next film, Intermezzo, Howard would be the associate producer as well as the star.

The right combination had been found and the tumblers turned smoothly. Unfortunately, the bait was never to be delivered. Delays in the shooting of Gone With the Wind left Howard with no time to perform the producing functions that were so appealing to him on Intermezzo. Indeed, he barely had time to appear in the film.

To one woman
he gave his memories...
to another
he gave his dreams—
wild longings—
fierce desires
he dared not name...
for an interlude of
stolen love!
Could any woman
be content with
half a love?
Could any man
summon enough
for both?...
A vivid portrayal by

LESLIE HOWARD

star player extraordinary in

INTERMEZZO
A Love Story

SELZNICK INTERNATIONAL'S
great production introducing
the glamorous new Swedish star

INGRID BERGMAN

Produced by DAVID O. SELZNICK
Leslie Howard, Associate Producer
Released thru United Artists

In this ad for Intermezzo, *producer Selznick does an unusual thing—*
he displays the name of his Associate Producer, Mr. Leslie Howard.

With Ingrid Bergman in
Intermezzo (1939)

Howard found himself acting
in both Gone With the Wind
and Intermezzo
simultaneously, darting from
one sound stage to another,
switching costumes on the
way—changing from the
idealistic Southerner to the
idealistic violinist.

Many were called and few were chosen from the galaxy of stars who were tested and weighed for the four starring roles in Gone With the Wind. Winners and losers alike stared out at the moviegoing public from the covers of America's fan magazines.

SCREEN STARS

June—15¢

Susan Hayward

Exclusive GREER GARSON Interview by May Mann

PHOTOPLAY
combined with
MOVIE MIRROR

SEPTEMBE

OLIVIA de HAVILLAND
BY PAUL HESSE

48
26

MODERN SCREEN

OW TO WIN DATES AND INFLUENCE SWAINS — HOLLYWOOD'S FOOLPROOF TECHNIQUE!

FEBRUARY
10
CENTS

VIVIEN LEIGH'S & LAURENCE OLIVIER'S
LATEST SCREEN HIT
IN COMPLETE STORY FORM!
ALSO
MATRIMONIAL CHART AND
PERSONAL DATA ON
SCREEN STARS

VIVIEN
LEIGH

PHOTOPLA

HOLLYWOOD'S
FASHION
AUTHORITY

FEBRUARY

CLARK GABLE
By Paul Hesse

New! COMPLETE IN THIS ISSUE
Movie Book of the Month

WE ARE NOT ALONE
BY JAMES HILTON

THE NOVEL
ON WHICH THE
PAUL MUNI FIL
IS BASED

ONLY 5 CENT MOVIE MAGAZINE IN THE WORLD
A FAWCETT PUBLICATION

Hollywood
NOVEM

5c

TRY THE
LORETTA YOUNG
"REGULAR GUY"
TEST ON YOUR
BOY FRIEND

SEE
PAGE
25

MYRNA LOY'S TIRED OF BEING A WIFE!

MODERN SCREEN

THE LARGEST CIRCULATION OF ANY SCREEN MAGAZINE

Gay! Intimate! Unexpected!

PHOTOPLAY

5¢   MARCH

A personal story on **Clark Gable** *by Adela Rogers St. Johns*

movie MIRROR

MARCH
10¢
MACFADDEN PUBLICATION

SHEARER and GABLE TAKE A DARE!

Behind The Scenes With
"IDIOT'S DELIGHT"
Hollywood's Boldest Challenge

THE SECRET CORRESPONDENCE OF ERROL FLYNN
IF DEANNA DURBIN WERE MICKEY ROONEY'S GIRL

SCREEN STARS

FEBRUARY 15¢

PAULETTE GODDARD

HOLLYWOOD'S MOST THRILLING MAGAZINE

PHOTOPLAY

HOLLYWOOD'S FASHION AUTHORITY

OLIVIA DE HAVILLAND
By Paul Hesse

"LOVE AND THE LEADING LADIES"
By ED SULLIVAN

Silver Screen

10c

April

Miriam Hopkins

CLARA BOW SHOWS HER SPUNK Page 22

Silver Screen

JANUARY

10c

JANET GAYNOR in
"Tess of the Storm Country"

MODERN SCREEN

THE LARGEST CIRCULATION OF ANY SCREEN MAGAZINE

JUNE
10 CENTS

VIVIEN LEIGH

"DON'T CALL ME A GREAT LOVER!"
INSISTS
LAWRENCE OLIVIER

THE OTHER LIBERATED WOMAN

Psychologists would say that the tremendous appeal of Gone With the Wind *lay in the fact that Scarlett O'Hara was the first truly liberated woman. Every woman who read of the feverish, feisty Scarlett and how she manipulated the men in her life, must have grudgingly admired her spirit in the face of personal and historical crisis.*

There is a curious paradox to the liberation of Scarlett O'Hara, for she was the creation of a woman to whom liberation was traumatic. The fame that Gone With the Wind *brought Margaret Mitchell, as a novel and as a film, was a threat to be avoided at all costs. She refused to participate in the film's production. She declined to write the screenplay. She refused to examine the work of Sidney Howard. She turned her back on the search for Scarlett. She avoided expressing a preference in the casting.*

Margaret Michell had

Margaret Mitchell, novelist

always shunned the spotlight. Indeed, when a Macmillan editor had first inquired about the manuscript she was writing about the Civil War, she heatedly denied that such a manuscript even existed. When her husband, advertising man John Marsh, finally persuaded his wife to entrust the manuscript to the Macmillan emissary, she wired the editor the following day to demand its return. She had changed her mind, she said.

But when the book became an overnight sensation, a Book of the Month Club selection, a Pulitzer Prize winner, and a titanic motion picture, the limelight that threatened to engulf Margaret Mitchell left her stunned and frightened.

During the forty-eight years of her life, Peggy Marsh (née Margaret Mitchell) seemed a most improbable person to create the first thoroughly liberated woman of American fiction.

She was a very private woman whose outgoing nature was confined to Atlanta's social scene. When she badly sprained an already injured ankle and was turned into a virtual invalid, her husband suggested that she work on the novel she had often discussed. And so, primarily to appease him, Margaret Mitchell set to work writing a novel of magnolias and cotton and war.

Margaret Mitchell rejected the independence of the limelight, preferring the path of Melanie. She had the perception to picture a rebellious, independent woman, without having the stomach to become one.

◀ **GUTTED PLANTATION.**

When she was barely ten, Peggy Marsh and her mother rode a horse and buggy through the gently rolling Georgian hills. Young Peggy observed the ruins of ravaged plantations and scorched earth. As the wheels turned, the ghost of this dead civilization took hold of her. It was a ghost that would be exorcised by her monumental novel.

SCARLETT O'HARA.

The moviegoing public came very close to following the frenzied life of a Southern belle named Pansy O'Hara. That was the name Margaret Mitchell first gave her heroine. But as the years passed and Margaret Mitchell wrote and rewrote her only novel, Pansy turned to Scarlett. No doubt the name Scarlett seemed better to suit her heroine's fiery temperament.

RHETT BUTLER.

Though the names of Scarlett and Tara changed as the author wrote and refined her magnum opus, one name had a proper ring to it and remained unchanged from the beginning. It combined two of the most familiar names in Charleston, and in combination had the perfect sound: Rhett Butler.

TARA.

When Margaret Mitchell first created the venerable Southern mansion that was home to the O'Hara clan, she called it Fountenoy Hall. As the months passed, Fountenoy Hall turned simply to Tara. For this change, composer Max Steiner would be forever grateful. What resonance would there be in a musical composition called "Fountenoy's Theme"?

AFTER THE RAID.

Peggy Marsh leapfrogged about the novel, writing chapters out of sequence, plunging forward in time, then retreating to an earlier event. It was a scant three months before her book was released that she decided how to dispose of Scarlett's stolid second husband, Frank Kennedy. She determined that dear old Frank would die in a Ku Klux Klan raid triggered by a Negro's attack on Scarlett.

◄ **SCARLETT'S FIRST HUSBAND.**

At the age of eighteen, Peggy Mitchell was engaged to a second lieutenant in General Pershing's expeditionary force. Soon after their engagement was announced, the young man sailed for France where he died in battle. Scarlett marries young Charles Hamilton who leaves for war shortly after their wedding. Lieutenant Hamilton dies on the battlefield too, though of measles, not of shrapnel.

ATLANTA BAZAAR.

Scarlett brings gasps to the doyennes of Atlanta when, still clad in her widow's weeds, she bouyantly dances with Rhett Butler in the famous Atlanta bazaar scene. Peggy Mitchell had brought gasps to the doyennes of Atlanta when, shortly after her mother's passing, she danced with abandon at a charity ball. The stares of those society matrons must have been fresh in her mind when Margaret Mitchell described Scarlett's little rebellion.

WOUNDED SOLDIERS.

When Margaret Mitchell began work on her novel, she plowed through the military records of the Confederate Army to learn their tactics, triumphs and tragedies. Among the records of the South's Medical Corps, she found the grim facts she needed to describe the massive open-air hospital that Scarlett encounters on the Atlanta street.

THE SEARCH FOR SCARLETT - PART II

The pious say that when God closes a door, He opens a window. The impious say that when the going gets tough, the tough get going. Both observations were borne out by David Selznick's strategy when he was faced with a two-year delay in the filming of Gone With the Wind.

To acquire the services of Clark Gable, Selznick was forced to give MGM full distribution rights to his film. Since Selznick's company had a binding contract with United Artists to distribute his films, this meant a two-year delay in the commencement of production until the contract expired.

Selznick promptly turned lemons into lemonade. Faced with the herculean task of keeping the nation's attention for two years, he came up with the notion of a nationwide hunt to discover an unknown to play the role of Scarlett.

Thus, Selznick would appeal to the evergreen notion that superstars can be found in any candy store and at every checkout counter. He would provide reporters and columnists with the raw material from which miles of copy would flow.

It was not that Selznick wanted an unknown for such a demanding role. The prospect of finding a fiery flower blossoming in some village hamlet seemed most improbable. David Selznick did not believe in the tooth fairy. But as a publicity scheme it was inspired.

Selznick had the perfect instrument for his plan. He had recently hired a reporter named Russell Birdwell as his studio's public relations chief. Formerly a police reporter for Hearst's Los Angeles Examiner, Birdwell had a taste for the audacious. So when Selznick proposed his bogus search for Scarlett, the publicity men embraced the scheme. For a complete unknown to play the most galvanic role in contemporary literature was enough to whet the appetite of the most callous editor. Some girl in Charleston or Tampa—or, God forbid, Boston—would enjoy instant fame.

Russell Birdwell deployed his press agents and casting agents to the four corners of the land. It was a noisy and even dangerous odyssey. Often the searchers barely escaped alive in the riotous receptions of Southern hopefuls.

Socialites, sales clerks, college girls, actresses with the most meager credentials—all were seriously read for the role of Scarlett, and their performances studiously reported in the local press.

The search yielded thousands of inches of newspaper space, acres of magazine articles, a flood of wire photos, and a shower of snapshots of Scarlett hopefuls, many of them fully costumed.

For the moviegoing public it was a Cinderella story in the making. For Selznick and

Director George Cukor interviews Louisa Robert of Atlanta, Susan Fallingant of Allentown, and Alicia Rhett of Charleston for the role of Scarlett.

Director Cukor tests Katherine Locke for the role of Melanie, and Lenore Ulric for the role of Belle Watling.

Photoplay *provides a sketch to help the searchers locate the ideal Scarlett.*

Birdwell it was maximum press at minimum cost.

Predictably, Selznick's much ballyhooed search produced no one who could be remotely considered for the role of Scarlett, and toward the end of his marathon ploy, certain astute members of the press began to smell the greasepaint behind the roar of the crowd. But by then the fires of Atlanta were burning brightly in Culver City.

The naïveté with which public and press accepted the pleasant fiction that an unknown was being sought for the longest role in motion picture history tends to support P. T. Barnum's observation about the birthrate of the gullible.

THE CINDERELLA HOAX

There could be no further delay.

Under the terms of his contract with MGM, Selznick had to put Gable to work by mid-February 1939. By December of 1938 Selznick had still not decided on an actress to play Scarlett—but production had to begin.

David Selznick planned to construct Tara on the back lot of the Pathé studio. He decided to clear away the vintage sets that were standing there by assembling them into a replica of old Atlanta and sending them up in flames. In this way he would clear the ground for Tara and shoot his Burning of Atlanta Scene in one fell swoop. Doubles for Scarlett and Rhett would ride a wagon through the inferno as the cameras rolled. The date was set for the second burning of Atlanta—December 11, 1938.

And still no Scarlett.

The night of the fire was cold. The Technicolor cameras were positioned to cover the blaze. The doubles were ready. An elevated platform had been erected for Selznick to oversee the fire. Brother Myron was expected; he was dining with some clients. When he was delayed, David Selznick could wait no longer.

He gave the signal and instantly the city of Atlanta—formed of the sets of King Kong and other Selznick films—began to blaze.

When the fire finally started to wane, Myron arrived, slightly drunk, with his dinner guests—actor Laurence Olivier and an attractive young woman.

David Selznick looked past his brother at the girl. The dying flames lit up the pale green eyes that Margaret Mitchell had described in her novel. Selznick took one look and knew that he had found his Scarlett.

A thrilling climax to a two-year search. The end of an odyssey for Selznick, the end of the rainbow for Vivien Leigh. Scarlett rising out of the ashes of Atlanta. Cinderella reborn in an eleventh-hour discovery.

Except it never happened.

Vivien Leigh had a barrister husband and an infant child when she appeared in her first film. It was a small role in a trivial comedy called Things Are Looking Up. A few more films followed, like trees falling in a remote forest, and then a play called The Mask of Virtue. The London critics were pleased. So was British filmmaker Alexander Korda, who saw the play, read the reviews and placed the lady under contract.

Korda put his young find in a historical drama called Fire over England. She made the most of it . . . both professionally and romantically. For Vivien met another cast member named Laurence Olivier and one of the most famous love affairs of the century began.

Vivien's screen career accelerated. She appeared

With Robert Taylor in A Yank at Oxford *(1938)*

again with Olivier in The First and the Last, *she captured Rex Harrison in* Storm in a Teacup, *and she cringed at Conrad Veidt in* Dark Journey.

Vivien was a woman on the move. MGM had reached out a tentacle from Culver City to Denham, England. Robert Taylor was to make a film there called A Yank at Oxford and Vivien was awarded the role of the adulterous wife. Her fiery qualities were well displayed opposite the stolid

Taylor. More important, Vivien was finally in the big league. A Yank at Oxford *was exhibited around the world. The little fish in a small pond had become a little fish in a very big one.*

When Margaret Mitchell's novel about a Southern minx hit the bestseller lists and David Selznick optioned the book for the screen, Vivien was determined to land the role. A British actress to play the Southern belle was the farthest thing from Selznick's

mind. But Vivien was undeterred. One of her countrymen, an aging playwright named George Bernard Shaw, had observed: "Some people see things as they are and ask 'Why?' I see things that never could be and ask 'Why not?' "

Vivien asked herself: "Why not Scarlett?"

She was unknown, English, and competing with half the stars in Hollywood. Still she was determined.

Vivien's agent was Harry

With Laurence Olivier in Fire over England (1936)

With Rex Harrison in Partners of the Night *(1937)*
With Conrad Veidt in Dark Journey *(1937)*

Ham, the British associate of agent Myron Selznick. Vivien directed the dubious Ham to propose her to Myron Selznick for the coveted role of Scarlett.

Unknown to Vivien, David Selznick had been secretly screening her British films at his hilltop home in Malibu and had already decided that this obscure English actress would make the ideal Scarlett. But it would not do to let the public and press know that he had fixed his mind on a Scarlett. It would arouse the enmity of the Hollywood actresses who thought they were still in the running. And it would put an end to the miles of type that the press was lavishing on his talent search. So Selznick kept his own counsel.

Selznick's decision on Vivien Leigh became a fiercely held secret and formed the basis for a gigantic public deception. He had secretly obtained copies of all of Vivien Leigh's English films and, in secret communiqués, urged Olivier and Leigh to postpone any plans for their divorces until his master work was launched.

Selznick then began secret discussions with Alexander Korda on the subject of Vivien Leigh. The actress, meanwhile, was cautioned not to mention Selznick's interest to anyone.

When Korda proved intransigent about selling Vivien's contract, Selznick was forced to look elsewhere for his Scarlett. But it was clear that his heart was in the highlands, with Vivien Leigh.

By late 1938, two years of relentless readings lay behind him, and Selznick turned back to Korda and Vivien Leigh. As so often happens with insurmountable obstacles, the passage of time had worn them away. Laurence Olivier had established himself in Hollywood and was about to begin shooting Wuthering Heights with Merle Oberon. Korda realized it would help Olivier's box office if the actor's paramour were to become better known to Americans. Korda knew of Vivien's lust for the Scarlett role, and so he turned from an antagonist to a willing conspirator.

Thus began the Cinderella Hoax.

Vivien Leigh set sail for America. The journey was heavy with intrigue. The press was informed, in the most offhanded way possible, that the actress had expectations of taking the place of Merle Oberon in Wuthering Heights. This was about as likely as Mickey Rooney relacing Louis B. Mayer as head of MGM. But the press dutifully reported the story. From New York, Vivien flew to Los Angeles, taking care to avoid newsmen and movie executives.

Arriving in Hollywood, the master plan called for Vivien to keep a low profile. Her discovery must be carefully orchestrated.

It was determined that Myron Selznick would bring the actress to the Selznick lot just as the flames began leaping skyward in the Burning of Atlanta Scene. There, with the reflection of the flames dancing in Vivien's cool green eyes, David Selznick would discover his Scarlett—and the American public would have a fairy-tale climax to the historic search.

But the best laid hoaxes can go awry. Vivien and Olivier appeared at the Selznick studio promptly on cue. But where was Myron? All the players had to be assembled for the charade, and one of the key performers was missing. Unwilling to wait any longer, David Selznick gave the signal for the burning of Atlanta to begin.

Gallons of fuel fed the fire, flames leaped hundreds of feet in the air, and the ersatz city of Atlanta turned to ashes.

Finally Myron Selznick arrived—and he was in his cups. But like the professional he was, Myron played the classic scene faultlessly. The dying flames illumined the pale green eyes that Margaret Mitchell had described.

David Selznick took one look and knew that he had found his Scarlett . . .

Cut and print.

America had its Cinderella story and Selznick had his Scarlett.

THE COMING OF VIVIEN LEIGH

SHE'S SCARLETT O'HARA

And now at last you can read the real reason for the delays in selecting the characters in the cast of the century!

By Elizabeth Wilson

Scarlett O'Hara was a household word. Vivien Leigh was an unknown. From the day that David Selznick announced that Vivien would play Scarlett, it was necessary to correct the disparity in their fame. This was the job of the fan magazines, the company press of the motion picture industry.

I CAN'T help lying awake nights and worrying over what is going to happen to Hollywood dinner conversation—now that "Gone With the Wind" is cast. What in God's nightgown, as *Scarlett* used to say, are people going to talk about now? I can't recall facing a bowl of soup that someone didn't crack out with, "Who is going to play *Scarlett?*" With the roast lamb and mint sauce came Katharine Hepburn; Bette Davis arrived with the string beans and carrots, and Margaret Sullavan accompanied the mashed potatoes. "I won't go near it if Jean Arthur plays *Scarlett!*" . . . "Paulette Goddard! My dear, the South would sue." . . . "If Miriam Hopkins gets it I'll leave town" . . . etc., etc., etc.

Such a clatter of indignant shrieks and yells while the poor movie star hostess looks on in pained surprise. "I," she mutters to herself, "am the only actress in Hollywood who can play *Scarlett*. Can't a one of these dopes realize that?" I'm telling you that by the time the coffee arrived no one would be speaking to anyone else. No wonder I have indigestion.

. . . ll, what with the dollar where it is now, and I'm

sure I don't even *know* where it is, I don't get about the country much; but my friends who travel tell me that dinner conversations, followed by fisticuffs and free-for-alls, have been the same in Georgia, Kansas, Nebraska and New England ever since that dreadful summer of 1936 when David Selznick dropped a bomb-shell. Never have people had so much to say on any subject as they have on who is to play *Scarlett*. And poor Mr. Selznick contends that never have people had so much to *write* on any subject as they have on who is to play *Scarlett*. So now that *Scarlett* is cast, and the fun is over, and my digestion is getting better daily, thank you, I think it might be interesting to hold a post mortem and clear up a few of those casting mysteries.

In the summer of 1936 David Selznick, of Selznick International Pictures, through a New York agent, Annie Laurie Williams, bought the movie rights to a book written by Margaret Mitchell of Atlanta, Georgia, and

"Scarlett O'Hara"

BEGS AMERICA TO GIVE HER A CHANCE

BY HAROLD KEENE

Here they are—all three winners in the big "Gone With the Wind" sweepstakes! Left to right are Vivien ("Scarlett," of course), Leslie Howard ("Ashley"), and Olivia de Havilland ("Melanie").

Have a heart! Vivien Leigh, the English girl chosen for the role, faces a tougher battle than the little Southern girl ever knew!

THE breakfast tea that innumerable gentlemen's gentlemen serve each morning to the Bertie Woosters of the world comes from Darjeeling, India; and from Darjeeling, of all places, came some twenty years ago the little English girl whom, within a few months, millions of people will see and know as Scarlett O'Hara.

She was five, then, and innocent of her destiny. Maybe, before the year is out, she will wish fervently and with prayer that she were back in Darjeeling again; indeed, that she had never left the place. Because it is likely that even with David Selznick's improbable two-year campaign of public enlightenment, Darjeeling has not yet heard of Margaret Mitchell or "Gone With the Wind" or the fantastic controversy over Who Should Play Scarlett, which—to the exclusion of wars and the fall of nations—has occupied American thought and energy for so long.

She is small and trim and excitingly lovely, this Vivien Leigh, with a personality like the swish of

Before passing judgment, be sure to read Vivien's fascinating history—you'll be surprised! Remember, too, how she captured American hearts in "A Yank at Oxford," with Bob Taylor (below). Isn't it likely she'll do at least as well, with Clark Gable?

neighborhood theater when at long last its marquee reads, "Gone With the Wind."

You have, on the whole, been a little angry ever since the first announcement of the final choice was made. You have said, on your personal stationery, that it was certainly a fine state of affairs that an Englishwoman should be Scarlett O'Hara when there were innumerable Southern girls—at least *American* girls—who could do the job so well. "Why not cast Chiang Kai Shek," you have said with mirthless humor, "as Gerald O'Hara? And Lupe Velez as Ellen?"

You have said, "Is Selznick *crazy?*"

But if you are still saying these things it is because you have not watched the slight figure of Vivien Leigh, inexpressibly tired from four-

---

HEIGH-HO, SCARLETT!

BY DALE EDWARDS

Vivien says she's qualified to play a southerner because her last name—Leigh—is pronounced just like our Robert E. Lee's.

Meet the English girl who plays a southern belle

Laurence Olivier and Vivien are said to be "that way." They met making a picture.

Clark Gable and Vivien in "Gone With The Wind." Rumor had 'em not speaking.

HEIGH-HO, Scarlett! Heigh-ho, Vivien Leigh! How are yuh, honey chile? And how, after five months of playing Scarlett, are yuh bearing up? What about those nasty cracks that were made about an English gal playing that southern che-ild? Say, are you-all steamed up about them? Meet Vivien Leigh. Meet a small, slim, beauteous girl with a personality like a slumbering volcano, which may erupt at any moment, and an English accent that sounds as if it came right out of Oxford. Her southern accent, ma'am? She can turn that melting accent—learned from Susan Myrick, the Emily Post of the South—on and off like a faucet.

Recently, I talked to Vivien Leigh and became aware of the quality in her that led David Selznick to give her the role of Scarlett in preference to all the glamorous, beautiful Hollywood actresses who would have given their artificial eyelashes for the part.

If you have read "Gone With The Wind," it is a waste of time to describe her. For she is so much like Scarlett O'Hara, that she might have been torn from the pages of the novel. Consider Margaret Mitchell's description of Scarlett: "Scarlett O'Hara was not beautiful, but men seldom realized it when caught by her charm as the Tarleton twins were. In her face were too sharply blended the delicate features of her mother, a Coast aristocrat of

French descent, and the heavy ones of her florid Irish father. But it was an arresting face, pointed of chin, square of jaw. Her eyes were pale green without a touch of hazel, starred with bristly black lashes and sharply tilted at the ends."

Substitute, in this description, the name of Vivien's husband, Leigh Holman, in place of the Tarleton twins (or the name of Laurence Olivier, who has been rumored to be interested in her) and you have Vivien Leigh. Say that her mother was born in Ireland, and her father was a stockbroker of French descent, in India, and you have Vivien's ancestry straight. Her real name was Vivien Hartley Holman, and she was born in Darjeeling, India.

Though Vivien's simply dripping charm, there's a trace in her of Scarlett's ruthlessness. You have the distinct feeling that if ever her back were to the wall, she would put up a fiercer battle than any Scarlett ever fought. So far she has been on the spot only once, when she was chosen for the role of Scarlett. Had a bombshell been dropped by a foreign airship in the South, it couldn't have resulted in more excitement and bitterness.

The Osceola, Florida, Chapter of the United Daughters of the Confederacy passed a motion to boycott "Gone With The Wind" because of the selection of Vivien Leigh. Southern gentlemen wrote impassioned letters to the newspapers, in which they said, "The selection of Vivien

Leigh is a direct affront to the men who wore the Gray and an outrage to the memory of the heroes of 1776 who fought to free this land of British domination."

The grandson of a Confederate soldier wrote, "Cheer for the Osceola Chapter of the Daughters and more power to their boycott of the film. It is high time those Hollywood producers found out that there are still those to whom the honor of southern womanhood is not just an empty phrase."

Faced with such a storm of criticism, some actresses would have resigned from the role. But Vivien Leigh said, shrugging her slim shoulders, "I was not at all upset or annoyed by the criticism. Why should I be? When an English girl is signed for such a typically American part, it is obvious that there will be comment. And even the worst comments were no worse than I expected!"

The press agent suggested at this point that all those nasty comments acted as a challenge to Vivien, and to this Vivien smilingly agreed.

"It was a terrific strain making 'Gone With The Wind,'" she confessed, "and toward the end our nerves were all shot. And no wonder! We worked under three different directors, first George Cukor, then Victor Fleming and finally, Sam Wood. No sooner did we get used to the ideas of one director than a new one was brought in, and we had to learn to work with each in turn."

George Cukor resigned when he couldn't agree with David Selznick as to how the script should be handled, and then Victor Fleming was brought in. When he became ill, Sam Wood, who directed "Goodbye Mr. Chips," took his place.

"Did you have to change your characterization of Scarlett each time?" I asked Vivien.

She lifted that strange, defiant face, and her jaw looked squarer than ever.

"I didn't change my characterization," she said. "I just had to get used to working with different directors, but my characterization is my characterization, and I wouldn't change it for anyone."

That's the Scarlett O'Hara in her.

And what's *her* characterization of Scarlett?

"I admired her tremendously, but at the same time I was furious with her for being so hard and selfish, and when Rhett Butler left her, I felt she had gotten exactly what she deserved. If her mother had lived or if she had allowed herself to come under the influence of Rhett Butler, she might have been a different girl. But because Rhett Butler was so much like her—though in a much nicer way—she didn't realize how right he was for her, but was interested in Ashley, who was completely wrong for her."

She firmly denies that any feud (Continued on page 93)

THE SON-IN-LAW ALSO RISES

In recent years we have heard much about the auteur theory of filmmaking. The director, we are told, is the man who puts his stamp on a motion picture. Back in the thirties the director was just a hired hand and it was the producer who was the man in charge. But the producer generally did not have sufficient creative juices or executive clout to place his stamp on a film. The studio head and the system itself were too strong.

There is one glowing exception to this lack of creative control—a producer who exemplified the auteur theory of filmmaking at work—and that man was David Selznick.

As a boy, David Selznick was in awe of the movie business that his father had pioneered. But when Lewis Selznick's kingdom crumbled—when he was struck down by the Hollywood moneychangers— young David was trans-

formed into an avenging lion, determined to raise the Selznick name to new heights.

David and his brother Myron were left penniless when their father's movie empire collapsed into bankruptcy. In their young manhood, David and Myron moved to Hollywood.

Myron sought his own road in avenging his father. He became a Hollywood agent. Contriving to represent the top actors, directors and screenwriters in town, he soon tripled their income by gouging larger and larger fees from the men who had brought down his father.

David's road to revenge was more ironic. He would defeat the movie moguls by becoming one of them. By 1931 David Selznick had become production chief at RKO Studios and married the daughter of the head of MGM, Louis B. Mayer, despite the old man's violent objections. He had also made his name more imposing in

the manner later employed by Harry Truman. He added a middle initial.

But David O. Selznick was not the sort of fraudulent climber Budd Schulberg described in his angry indictment of Hollywood, What Makes Sammy Run? Sammy Glick was a ruthless, shallow young man, naked of talent and scruples. Selznick may have shared Sammy's ambitions, but he was a man of taste and creative acumen.

Within a year after taking over the reins at RKO, Selznick had released two films that would prove critically and financially successful. One was about a giant ape called King Kong. The other was a show-business story called What Price Hollywood. He selected a man named George Cukor to direct it.

The success of What Price Hollywood formed a bond between producer and director that would eventually lead Selznick to choose

Cukor to direct the very gem of his career. For the moment, he tapped Cukor to direct A Bill of Divorcement. Selznick had misgivings about the strident young actress that Cukor wanted for the lead, but he bowed to his director's choice. And so was launched the career of Katharine Hepburn. Selznick's foray into the classics commenced when he, Cukor and Hepburn next joined forces in the RKO production of Little Women.

Meanwhile, at his Culver City duchy, Louis B. Mayer was having his differences with his own resident genius, Irving Thalberg. When the sickly Thalberg left for Europe after a heart attack, Mayer invited Selznick to take up residence on the MGM lot. Selznick's box-office successes at RKO had mellowed the old man toward his outspoken son-in-law. Selznick promptly accepted the offer. And so, in 1933 David Selznick came willingly to the studio to which a few years later he would be dragged, kicking and screaming.

Selznick set out to exploit the constellation of stars in the Metro galaxy. He optioned a play by George Kaufman and Edna Ferber called Dinner at Eight and poured into it virtually every star on the lot. Nothing succeeds like excess and Dinner at Eight emerged a smash hit.

Selznick went where the heat was. He starred Clark Gable in Dancing Lady, and when the King delivered a resounding hit, starred him again in Manhattan Melodrama. Success again. Selznick was now sitting squarely in the catbird seat. His options were open, his leverage increasing.

He turned to the classics, He would make a film of David Copperfield. But his father-in-law was opposed. The classics were lousy box office, said Mayer with some justification. But Mayer's opposition proved as futile as it had been to his daughter's marriage. Mayer gave David Copperfield his grudging approval. The two Davids were triumphant—the film was a resounding hit.

As Selznick's career blossomed, he was developing work habits that his friends would call decisive and his detractors call tyrannical. Those work habits became a legend in Hollywood. It was said that he consumed people, that he burned them out. It was said he could leave nothing to subordinates. His energy carried him into every area of filmmaking from script to hairdressing. He approved every syllable of a script and wrote eighty percent of it himself.

Selznick was an eloquent man with a roving mind that made the writing of memos a sensible means of conveying

his views to employees without the necessity of hearing their rebuttal. As Selznick supervised his various films, he poured out a torrent of words to a pair of alternating secretaries. Though his syntax often faltered, one feels on reading his memos that here is a mind teeming with facts and opinions. They make one think of a ship's captain tossing cargo overboard in order to pick up speed.

The Selznick memos also help explain the success of Gone With the Wind, which now lay on the horizon. They explain how one man was able to bring together in a complex, collaborative medium a thousand artists and technicians, and despite changes in directors, writers, cameramen, editors and actors, produce a film of such flawless unity.

By the time Irving Thalberg returned to MGM, Selznick had established himself with several emphatic hits. He was now determined to run the show himself. He knew, of course, that he could not do so with Mayer in the front office and Thalberg at his elbow. So, with the financial backing of Jock Whitney and a portfolio of other blue-chip investors, he formed Selznick International. In a little over a year, David had produced six films under his own banner. The longevity of their appeal testifies to Selznick's touch

Selznick

King Kong *(1933)*

Little Women *(1933)*

Manhattan Melodrama *(1934)*

Viva Villa *(1934)*

A Star Is Born *(1937)*

Dancing Lady *(1933)*

Dinner at Eight *(1933)*

David Copperfield *(1935)*

Anna Karenina *(1935)*

Little Lord Fauntleroy *(1936)*

Nothing Sacred *(1937)*

The Adventures of Tom Sawyer *(1938)*

Gone With the Wind *(1939)*

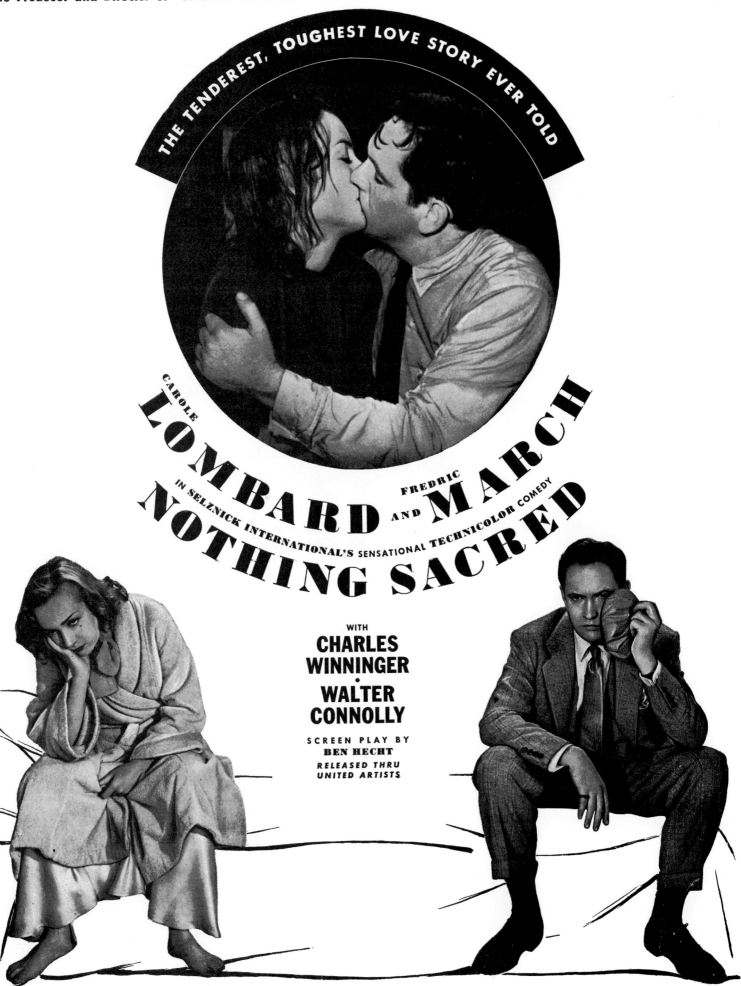

Ad for Nothing Sacred *(1937)*

78

A SON...
PROUD OF HIS MOTHER

... worshipping the ground she walked on ... loving her with a fierce loyalty ... yet at the same time stealing his way into the flinty heart of a proud, tyrannical nobleman and teaching him the meaning of kindness.

Freddie Bartholomew breathes life into Frances Hodgson Burnett's beloved character, "Little Lord Fauntleroy" and gives a perform-

ance in the world-famous story that will indelibly stamp itself upon your heart. Dolores Costello Barrymore as "Dearest" his mother, returns to the screen lovelier and more radiant than ever. She will delight the millions of fans who have been eagerly awaiting her return.

We'd like to be modest in our statements about this picture — but

the facts speak for themselves ... It has a magnificent cast — a perfect story — was directed by John Cromwell who thrilled you with "Of Human Bondage" — produced by David O. Selznick who gave you "David Copperfield" and the screenplay was written by Hugh Walpole, noted English author.

It is a picture that is marked for major screen honors in 1936!

Selznick International Pictures, Inc., *Presents*

LITTLE LORD FAUNTLEROY
with
FREDDIE BARTHOLOMEW *and* **DOLORES COSTELLO BARRYMORE**
Mickey Rooney • C. Aubrey Smith • Guy Kibbee • Henry Stephenson
E. E. Clive • Una O'Connor • Jackie Searl • Ivan Simpson • Jessie Ralph
PRODUCED BY DAVID O. SELZNICK Released thru UNITED ARTISTS

Ad for Little Lord Fauntleroy *(1936)*

and talent—The Prisoner of Zenda, Little Lord Fauntleroy, Tom Sawyer, Nothing Sacred *and* A Star Is Born.

It will be seen that Selznick continued to rely on the works of literature for his motion pictures. Rather than depend on an original conception, he preferred to exploit the built-in audience and well-laid structure of an existing novel.

In 1936 a novel appeared that would change David Selznick's life for better and for worse.

Selznick's New York story editor, Kay Brown, sent her boss a summary of a lengthy historical novel that was still in galley form. It seems a diminutive Southern lady named Margaret Mitchell had been seduced into relinquishing her novel to an editor of the Macmillan Company, and according to Miss Brown, it had the makings of a spectacular motion picture. No doubt what appealed to the assertive Miss Brown was the novel's heroine, an assertive young woman named Scarlett O'Hara. Miss Brown urged her employer to drop everything and buy the rights. Her letter set in motion a series of events that would raise a hundred actors to new heights, dash many of them back to earth, and bequeath to the world the most popular movie ever made.

THE WOMAN'S DIRECTOR AND THE MAN'S DIRECTOR

Gone With the Wind *was the product of two directors who were mirror opposites of one another. The first was George Cukor, "the woman's director," a man of sensitivity and taste, who had directed Katharine Hepburn, Greta Garbo and Norma Shearer in their most evocative screen performances. When he was dismissed from* Gone With the Wind, *Vivien Leigh and Olivia de Havilland flew into producer Selznick's office and for three hours they beseeched, bullied and cajoled him to reinstate Cukor. When they were unsuccessful, they would each steal over to Cukor's home on weekends for his guidance in the week's upcoming scenes.*

The other director was Victor Fleming, "a man's director," hunter, flier and motorcycling buddy of Clark Gable who chose him to succeed Cukor. Fleming had never read the book, and thought the script an atrocity and the film a disaster. He was a man who could point to Vivien Leigh's *chest and snap at the costume designer, "For God's sake, let me see some boobs!" When asked by Miss Leigh how to play a certain scene, he could reply, "Just ham it up."*

These two very different men traveled very different roads to the film that would become the pinnacle of their careers.

Cukor's career in films began when sound invaded the movie capital bringing panic in its wake. He had demonstrated his talent for working with "talking" actors on the Broadway stage and thus captured the confidence of Hollywood filmmakers, an insecure lot at best, who were hysterical in the switch to sound.

Having come West, Cukor directed Tallulah Bankhead in Tarnished Angels, *controlling the lioness superbly. He caught the eye of a young moviemaker named David Selznick who was newly in power at RKO. This led to a contract and a kinship with the boy wonder.*

What Price Hollywood *was the first product of their collaboration, followed by* A Bill of Divorcement.

Cukor followed Selznick to the mammoth Metro studios where he directed some of the most prestigious films to emerge from Culver City, including Camille, The Women *and* The Philadelphia Story.

When David Selznick chose a director for Gone With the Wind, *Cukor seemed the inevitable choice. He seemed to have a talent for working with female stars. Virtually all his films had focused on females, and in the beginning Selznick perceived GWTW as primarily a film about a spirited young woman. It was only later that the epic scope of the film grew in Selznick's mind. It then seemed unwise to have it directed by a man whose forte was the delicate moment.*

But in the beginning Cukor seemed indispensable. Selznick conferred with him on the script and sent him south in search of locations.

Victor Fleming sets up a shot.

George Cukor directs a scene as Katharine Hepburn looks on.

Cukor was Selznick's right hand in all the pre-production work on Gone With the Wind. He tested hopefuls for the leading roles, labored over the evolving script, and worked with designer Menzies on sketches of every camera setup in the film.

For two years George Cukor was intimately involved in every aspect of Gone With the Wind. *Then two weeks into production, he was gone.*

The wags at the Brown Derby used to say: *"There's only one Clark Gable and that's Victor Fleming."* They would observe that the jug-eared farmboy seemed to be modeling his screen image after the man who directed him in Test Pilot and Red Dust—the man with whom he went drinking, motorcycling and womanizing.

Vic Fleming springboarded from a cameraman to a director of action films. His background made him a useful fellow in directing adventure films where facile camerawork was essential. When sound invaded Hollywood, Fleming held to the value of motion, refusing to be stifled by the demands of the ear over the eye.

MGM discovered Fleming in 1932 and promptly

Fleming adjusts his star's wardrobe.

84

Fleming prepares a scene on the Atlanta Street.

assigned him to a string of action films. Not for Fleming was the film of pathos. He directed such slam-bang vehicles as Captains Courageous and Test Pilot, the latter with Clark Gable.

Fleming was a man's director and a man's man. And in an industry where friendship spawns as many assignments as talent, his work proliferated from his association with Gable. The insecure star seemed comfortable with Fleming about. And between takes the wise-cracking, card-playing camaraderie of star and director provided a security blanket for the King.

Fleming was up to his hips in Munchkins on The Wizard of Oz set when the explosion occurred between Cukor and Selznick. The producer knew that Louis B. Mayer had run out of patience with Gone With the Wind. He would not permit any further delay. And MGM's Gable must be placated. Mayer insisted that one of Metro's contract directors replace Cukor.

Selznick brought the list of possible directors to Gable. It consisted of King Vidor, Robert Leonard, Jack Conway and Victor Fleming. Gable did not hesitate.

"Fleming, of course," he said.

THE REWRITING OF GONE WITH THE WIND

There is a classic comedy sketch about a movie producer and a screenwriter who are marooned on a desert island. The producer orders the writer to prepare a rescue note. The writer does so. The producer examines it and sadly shakes his head. "I'm sorry," says the producer, "but I'm going to have to call in another writer."

The novel Gone With the Wind was written by one person. The motion picture Gone With the Wind was written by seventeen. They included:

Sidney Howard, the Pulitzer Prize-winning playwright who wrote They Knew What They Wanted and The Silver Cord.

Ben Hecht, the facile playwright who coauthored The Front Page and Twentieth Century.

F. Scott Fitzgerald, the famous novelist who wrote The Great Gatsby and The Last Tycoon.

John van Druten, the gifted playwright who wrote I Remember Mama and The Voice of the Turtle.

Oliver H. P. Garrett, the screenwriter who wrote Manhattan Melodrama and Street of Chance.

Jo Swerling, the screenwriter who wrote Blood and Sand and The Westerner.

David Selznick, the producer of David Copperfield and King Kong.

Margaret Mitchell, who participated in the screenplay in the sense that virtually all of its dialogue was extracted from her novel.

In translating Margaret Mitchell's marathon tome to the screen, David Selznick first tapped Sidney Howard, a Broadway playwright with impeccable credits: a Pulitzer Prize for They Knew What They Wanted, The Silver Cord, Dodsworth. Selznick regarded Howard as one of only two outstanding screenwriters who were not locked to Hollywood studios. He was also a "businessman writer" who could be depended on to deliver a massive piece of work on a strict timetable.

Balanced against these virtues was a built-in problem. Sidney Howard preferred to work in seclusion at his Eighty-eighth Street Manhattan apartment. His working habits were those of the novelist who labors at his lonely gamble and turns in a finished work. Such behavior requires confidence and talent. Selznick, unfortunately, was the sort of producer who only felt thoroughly in control when he could hold daily meetings with his screenwriter, examine a daily output of pages, maintain a steady collaborative association. These daily meetings were not feasible with David in Culver City and his writer on East Eighty-eighth Street.

Howard began his herculean adaptation by meeting with Selznick in Hollywood, then hurried back to Manhattan to get to work.

The novel was by now familiar to millions and Selznick was wary of gutting it to make a film of manageable length. He computed that to bring the complete novel to the screen without omitting any scene in the book would require a 168-hour film. One would have to spend a week in his theatre seat. Who could endure such an epic?

Sidney Howard's work was cut out for him. As usual, he wrote at an extraordinary pace. Within the space of eight weeks, he had telescoped Margaret Mitchell's half million words to a trifling four hundred pages of movie script. It was a masterpiece of compression.

But four hundred pages would produce a six-hour movie, still very taxing to the modern moviegoer. Selznick's first thought was to produce a two-part film, to be viewed on separate evenings. Selznick was less afraid of breaking precedents than of damaging the property. But he encountered such violent objections from theatre owners that he discarded the idea of what would have become the world's first mini-series.

Instead he summoned Sidney Howard to Hollywood. Director Cukor joined them and the three men set to work trimming the script to a feasible length. This was no time for the marginal cuts of dialogue. Whole scenes had to go, and whole characters had to be ruthlessly pruned from the O'Hara family tree. Scarlett's child by her first marriage disappeared. Then the child of her second marriage. Following this literary infanticide, the Ku Klux Klan scenes were axed for political reasons.

Suddenly Selznick hit the ceiling. He discovered that Sidney Howard had actually inserted a scene in the screenplay that did not appear in the book! There is no accounting for the behavior of writers who want to write.

When Selznick, Howard and Cukor completed their sanguinary surgery, seventy pages had been lopped from Howard's four hundred. At this point, feeling his work was done and his money earned, Sidney Howard returned to New York. Selznick was furious at the playwright's attitude. A screenwriter should continue to rewrite a script until all the kinks were gone. The producer put the Howard screenplay on the shelf where it would remain until a year later when in the midst of production, Selznick would hunt desperately for this original product of talent and conciseness.

With Sidney Howard gone and his script out of favor, Selznick sought a more pliable screenwriter for Gone With the Wind. There is certainly no shortage of compliant screenwriters in Hollywood—Hollywood writers long ago bartered their independence for the good life. So Selznick found a malleable writer. The producer had worked with Oliver H. P. Garrett in his days at MGM and found him a resilient, reliable soul. Together Selznick and Garrett began rewriting the Sidney Howard scenario in a manner that seems borrowed from a Kaufman & Hart comedy—in the drawing room of a transcontinental train headed for New York.

Garrett was hampered—as were all the scenarists—by Selznick's obsession with Margaret Mitchell's prose. The producer continued to reiterate that the perfect screenplay for Gone With the Wind would not need a single original word. It would consist entirely of Miss Mitchell's dialogue, shuttled about in time and place. Garrett would sob with dismay when Selznick demanded a new scene, and the writer had to go scrabbling through the novel, borrowing lines from various chapters, to build the new scene. That is carpentry of a most exquisite type.

The screenwriters on GWTW had the life expectancy of a fruitfly. Garrett's longevity was typically brief. After fourteen days he was replaced by a playwright no less distinguished than Sidney Howard, John van Druten.

F. Scott Fitzgerald (left), novelist and screenwriter

The revolving door continued to spin as van Druten was replaced by Jo Swerling. His tenure would be even shorter than those of his predecessors.

As the writers came and went, with each one struggling to place his own stamp on the monumental script, Selznick was anxious to keep track of who had done what to whom. He initiated the practice that has since become a commonplace in the motion picture industry: printing each successive set of changes on different colored paper. A rainbow of dialogue poured out of the Selznick mimeograph machines and

very soon the script of GWTW looked like a sunset with stage directions. Cynics have observed that with many movies, the script is the most colorful part of the production. Not so with Gone With the Wind.

Next among Selznick's battalion of screenwriters was F. Scott Fitzgerald. The famous novelist was ten years beyond his fame, plagued by debts, tormented by an institutionalized wife, haunted by doubts of his failing gifts. Budd Schulberg paints a pathetic picture of Fitzgerald in his novel The Disenchanted, which describes the novelist's bitterness and self-doubt

while working on his next assignment, a trifling movie called Winter Carnival.

When Fitzgerald was assigned to work on GWTW, he seized the opportunity like a drowning man. Fitzgerald was eager to prove himself within a Hollywood studio, which is akin to Norman Mailer seeking self-esteem in a Chinese cooky factory.

Fitzgerald's rewrite was more a work of editing than of actual creation. He plowed through the script, blue-penciling page after page of what he deemed superfluous talk. This could not have been pleasant for Selznick, who had labored for months to distill the existing dialogue. Fitzgerald assessed the novel as "surprisingly good," but could not resist a word of condescension for those readers "who consider the book the supreme achievement of the human mind." By now most of Fitzgerald's own novels were long out of print.

Then, on the very eve of production, F. Scott Fitzgerald, author of Tender Is the Night and The Great Gatsby, was faced with a serious challenge. Director Cukor complained that Aunt Pitty was not funny enough. Miss Mitchell calls her quaint, the script calls her amusing, but she never actually says anything funny! Selznick ordered Fitzgerald to find some lines that would make Aunt Pittypat "funny."

Fitzgerald paced the producer's office long into the night, struggling to find some quaint, funny lines for Aunt Pitty. Alas, none of his suggestions satisfied Selznick. Fitzgerald was sent home, where a telegram from the studio awaited him. Fitzgerald was fired.

With the passage of time and the exhaustion of various screenwriters, a script was slowly emerging that was almost entirely the product of David O. Selznick. By the time shooting began, nearly every scene was either written or rewritten by the producer himself.

Selznick would work long into the night, rewriting the scenes to be shot the following day. This practice of eleventh hour creativity inevitably took its toll in the quality of the script. Or so the director felt.

George Cukor's complaints about the unplayability of these hastily written scenes led to his replacement by Victor Fleming. But to Selznick's dismay, Fleming was as critical of the script as was his predecessor.

Once more into the breech. One more rewrite was needed. Selznick turned to his friend Ben Hecht. Hecht was a brilliant if cynical show doctor who, like Sidney Howard, was spawned by the Broadway theatre. Unlike Howard, however, Hecht had developed an appetite for the luxuries of the Hollywood life. Hecht had written the entire screenplay for Selznick's Nothing Sacred in two weeks. He was fast and he was good. With the entire production of Gone With the Wind placed on "hold," Selznick needed Hecht and his terrible swift pen. The price was hastily negotiated. Hecht would receive $15,000 for a one week rewrite.

Selznick, Hecht and Fleming closeted themselves in the producer's office, surrounded by a squad of secretaries. Since neither Fleming nor Hecht had ever bothered to read the novel, Selznick spent an hour relating the convoluted story line. Both Hecht and Fleming found the story imcomprehensible. Hecht demanded to know if there wasn't somewhere a more coherent version of the screenplay. Selznick cast his mind back to the original screenplay that Sidney Howard had written in his Eighty-eighth Street apartment and that Selznick had shelved out of pique. After an hour-long search, the manuscript was unearthed.

Hecht found the Howard scenario to be a model of dramatic cohesion and announced that all it needed was some judicious editing. And so, for the rest of Hecht's $15,000 week, the three men set to work trimming the fat.

As Hecht edited the script, Selznick and Fleming acted out the scenes. Selznick played Scarlett and Fleming played Rhett, in a road-company version that cried to be preserved on film. The rewriting raced along. Hecht took a strong dislike to Ashley Wilkes and proposed that he be removed entirely. Cooler heads prevailed, but it challenges one to contemplate how Ben Hecht would have told Scarlett's story minus the man whose rejection drove her to lust, ambition and disaster.

In later years, when Selznick evaluated the contribution of each of his army of writers, he would say that Sidney Howard made the only tangible contribution. But he qualified this by observing that most of the format of the film was his own creation and that nearly all the dialogue was by Margaret Mitchell. Perhaps a handful of lines came from Hecht and van Druten. Period.

Ben Hecht, playwright and screenwriter

David O. Selznick, producer and screenwriter

It is not surprising to learn how much of the final script, in structure and syntax, was pure Selznick. In the collaborative business that is moviemaking, the screenwriter defers to the producer's wishes. As Ben Hecht observed, "Producers pay as much for obedience as they do for talent."

And as the legendary producer on the desert island said to his cringing scenarist, "I'm sorry, but I'm going to have to call in another writer."

SCENES FROM A MARRIAGE OF TALENTS

The motion picture is a peculiar art form. It consists of hundreds of individual scenes, filmed out of sequence over a period of many months, and then stitched together to form a coherent whole.

When one sits in a darkened theatre and views the parade of scenes that form Gone With the Wind and is swept along by its narrative power, one seldom thinks that each of the scenes had its own stormy history. Each is the result of a tortuous evolution in which a circle of strong-willed people exerted their influence on the shape and texture and the very survival of the scene. The novelist, the screenwriter, the producer, the director, the stars—each had his or her own perspective and often these perspectives were in sharp conflict with one another. Tensions and tussles took place and frequently change and compromise were the only solution.

Gone With the Wind

consisted of 684 scenes. Each of them posed its own problems. Here are some of them.

THE OPENING SCENE: in which Scarlett complains to the Tarleton twins of the talk of war.

The opening scene of the film was the first one shot. And reshot—and reshot

again. The rushes were dreadful. The hair of the Tarleton twins looked like corrugated rust. Scarlett's dress was a sickly green instead of a virginal white. The foliage looked false. The facade of Tara looked fake. With these minor exceptions, the scene was all a producer could wish to launch his epic film. The scene was shot again and again and again.

THE BARBECUE SCENE: in which Scarlett flirts with the men at the Wilkes Estate.

A scant week before production began, Selznick was still agonizing over the length of his script and preparing to eliminate some of the most memorable scenes in the novel. One of these was the Barbecue Scene. This sequence displayed Scarlett's flirtatiousness and her anger at the news of Ashley's engagement—but both of these had been established earlier on the porch. Selznick memoed Scott Fitzgerald: "The Barbecue Scene is completely unnecessary." The only possible reason to retain it was that readers might miss it. The scene remained.

MR. O'HARA'S WALK WITH SCARLETT: in which Scarlett and her father stroll across the Tara plantation.

Upon seeing the rushes, Selznick was shaken. With the sudden terror of 20-20 hindsight, Selznick feared that he should have made his movie on location. He must have been mad to put Tara on the back lot! The landscaping looked skimpy and false. Scarlett's father talks of the land being the only thing that matters, yet the land looked laughable.

Selznick fumed: "Tara looks like the backyard of a suburban home!" The producer belatedly decided that the back lot couldn't possibly reproduce the authentic charm of the Old South. And so he reshot the scene in Malibu.

**THE ATLANTA EXODUS:
in which Scarlett leaves
the hospital to discover that
Yankee cannon are pounding
Atlanta.**

*The streets of Atlanta are
clogged with citizens
evacuating the city. A
battalion of black laborers
marches through to dig
trenches for the Confederate
Army. The scene of chaos
had been carefully
choreographed by production
designer William Cameron
Menzies, and now Victor
Fleming was ready to film
Scarlett's intrepid double
running through the scene of
turmoil—the marching men,
frightened horses, rolling
wagons, exploding shells. But
Vivien Leigh said no. She
adamantly refused a double
for the scene. As the director
scowled and the insurance
representative chewed his
cuticle, Vivien Leigh strode
calmly through the exploding
shells.*

THE BURNING OF ATLANTA: in which Rhett leads a wagon bearing Scarlett, Melanie and her baby from the flaming city.

Before Tara and Twelve Oaks could be built on the back lot, a space had to be cleared for them. The area was crowded with the decaying sets of yesterday's movies—King Kong, Little Lord Fauntleroy, etc. It would take precious time to dismantle or move them. But Selznick had a better idea. He attached building facades to the vintage sets and sent them up in flames. He thus had his Burning of Atlanta Scene and a vacant back lot. It was an inspired idea. But there were minor complications. As the flames flew skyward and the cameras turned, some citizens of Culver City who knew nothing of the filming saw the orange ball of fire in the southern sky, assumed that Los Angeles was ablaze, climbed into their cars, and drove rapidly out of town!

THE BIRTH OF MELANIE'S
BABY: in which Scarlett
delivers Melanie's baby
amidst the siege of Atlanta.

When GWTW began
production, young Olivia de
Havilland had been neither a
wife nor a mother. Childbirth
was an alien experience, yet
she wanted to protray it
realistically. To prepare for
the scene, she spent hours
cowering in a corner of the
delivery room at Los Angeles
County Hospital. Olivia
observed that labor pains
were not continuous, but
came in waves. She informed
director Cukor of her findings
before shooting the scene,
and he repaid her research by
giving her ankle a painful
twist whenever he wanted her
to register a fresh cycle of
pain.

RHETT ENLISTS: in which Rhett Butler decides to enlist in the Confederate Army.

The most inexplicable enlistment in American literature occurs when Rhett Butler, cynic and opportunist, suddenly decides to enlist in the beaten, broken, Confederate Army. Director Cukor was appalled. The action is unmotivated. It is out of character and the audience would not believe it. How could he direct it to make it credible? Selznick had an answer. If just before he makes this decision, Rhett sees the heart-wrenching agony of a young Southern soldier, the audience may believe this sudden turnabout. And indeed they do. The profiteer sets out on his least profitable adventure with nary a raised eyebrow in the house.

THE YANKEE DESERTER SCENE: in which Scarlett kills a deserter who is bent on robbery and rape.

Selznick cast Paul Hurst in the part of the Yankee deserter. Hurst had been playing menacing heavies for over a decade. Sidney Howard was in favor of killing the scene instead of the deserter, but Selznick overruled him. When the scene was finally filmed, a sizable crowd of studio workers congregated on the sound stage. Paul Hurst thought it was a tribute to the tension of the scene. But there was a simpler explanation. In the scene, Melanie removes her nightgown to cover the dead soldier, and word had swept the studio that under her nightgown Olivia wore precisely nothing.

THE RECONSTRUCTION SCENE: in which a carpetbagger offers forty acres and a mule to some credulous blacks.

Sidney Howard wanted to create several new scenes that would portray the Reconstruction period and all its iniquities. To Selznick this was blasphemy. There was little enough time to use all the scenes that were pure Margaret Mitchell. To film additional scenes was unthinkable. Still, the Reconstruction could not be ignored. So Selznick shoehorned the Reconstruction into the existing scenes. For example, this glimpse of a carpetbagger and some susceptible blacks was inserted in the scene where Scarlett visits Rhett in an Atlanta prison.

THE PADDOCK SCENE:
in which Scarlett declares
her love for Ashley and
proposes that they run away
together.

It was the Paddock Scene that had secured the role for Vivien Leigh. In her screen test, she breathed a boldness into her performance of this scene that was the very essence of Scarlett. But when the day arrived to shoot the actual scene in the context of the film, it was like a pale fifth-carbon of the test. To make matters worse, Leslie Howard had lost interest in the role and kept forgetting his lines. Vivien urged director Fleming to look at her screen test. That was how the scene should look. Fleming did so, but when they reshot the scene the next day, it was still an anemic copy of the test.

THE PROPOSAL SCENE: in which Rhett Butler finally proposes marriage to Scarlett.

Most of the men who helped translate GWTW to the screen seem to have suffered from chauvinistic myopia. They perceived Scarlett as a selfish bitch. Vivien Leigh fought an abortive rearguard action to keep some trace of humanity in the character. In the scene in which Rhett proposes, the script has Scarlett reflect sadly: "My mother brought me up to be kind and thoughtful—and I've turned out such a disappointment." They are the words of an introspective, vulnerable woman. Selznick kept cutting them out of the script, and Vivien kept putting them back. Vivien won. The line, with its touch of humanity, survives.

RHETT POURS MAMMY A DRINK: in which Rhett toasts the birth of his new daughter.

After Scarlett gives birth to Bonnie Blue, an exultant Rhett pours a glass of Scotch for the usually abstemious Mammy. This is a red-letter day and the happy father wants to share his joy. As the cameras rolled, Rhett poured the cold tea that is the usual surrogate for Scotch in movie decanters. Hattie McDaniel said her line and gulped her drink. Suddenly she froze, gasped, and the set erupted with laughter. Gable had put real Scotch in the decanter.

THE MEASUREMENT SCENE: in which Scarlett discovers that motherhood has robbed her of her trim waistline.

Scarlett impulsively decides to have no more children and informs Rhett of her vow of abstinence. Vivien Leigh felt that the scene painted Scarlett as an unmitigated bitch. In the novel, it was much more than a widening waistline that prompted Scarlett to bar Rhett from her bed. It was a converstation with Ashley in which that vacillating Southern gentleman leads Scarlett to think he still loves her. Omitting this conversation makes Scarlett look shallow and Ashley look noble, a distortion of both their characters.

BONNIE AND THE MYSTERIOUS BREAKFAST TRAY:
in which Scarlett's daughter brings in her mother's breakfast.

Scarlett awakens after being bedded by a drunken Rhett. The scene opened as daughter Bonnie leaves, and the faithful Mammy enters to complain of her aches and pains to an oblivious Scarlett. But in the editing, the moment with Bonnie was cut from the film. Observant filmgoers will see Scarlet awaken with her glistening breakfast tray resting on her bed. They might speculate whether Rhett had actually called for a midnight snack.

LIGHTS, CAMERA, ACTION

David Selznick was an Orson Welles rolled into one. He used to say that "great films are made in their every detail according to the vision of one man." And that man was David Selznick. He was one of that rare breed of filmmakers who insist on making all the decisions. He insisted that every aspect of every creative element should be subject to his own sensibilities. His judgment would cover the smallest details of set design, costumes, music, editing, direction and script.

Selznick sensed that Gone With the Wind was the film that would mark his place in screen history. He marshaled an army of technicians, encouraged their creativity, but kept them on a short leash through the medium of his marathon memos. By the time he was through, he had produced a film to stand at the very pinnacle of the one-man movie.

What he failed to observe was that from such a pinnacle there is no place to go but down.

But such considerations were not apparent to Selznick when he was swept up in the project. Always an energetic man, Selznick now seemed charged by a fresh dynamo. His propensity for precise preparation reached its zenith. He demanded every aspect of design be absolutely authentic in script, sets and costumes.

His passion for authenticity drove him to hire one expert to validate Southern dialects, another to advise him on Southern etiquette, still another to advise him on Southern military strategy.

But however hard he drove his people, however obsessive his attention to detail, it should be recalled that in the end, Selznick had moved a battalion of artists to create the most popular motion picture of all time.

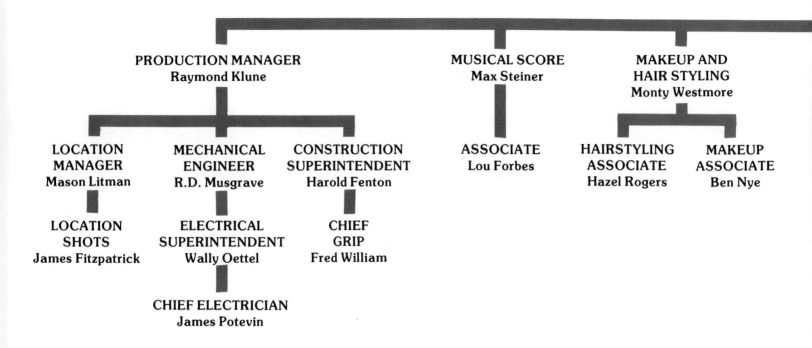

PRODUCTION MANAGER Raymond Klune			MUSICAL SCORE Max Steiner	MAKEUP AND HAIR STYLING Monty Westmore	
LOCATION MANAGER Mason Litman	MECHANICAL ENGINEER R.D. Musgrave	CONSTRUCTION SUPERINTENDENT Harold Fenton	ASSOCIATE Lou Forbes	HAIRSTYLING ASSOCIATE Hazel Rogers	MAKEUP ASSOCIATE Ben Nye
LOCATION SHOTS James Fitzpatrick	ELECTRICAL SUPERINTENDENT Wally Oettel	CHIEF GRIP Fred William			
	CHIEF ELECTRICIAN James Potevin				

Selznick dispatched a producer of travelogues to film backgrounds in the deep South, but the only material ever to reach the screen was a brief shot of a riverboat that was spliced into the Honeymoon Scene.

Selznick needed three hours of musical scoring on an incredibly tight deadline. When Max Steiner pleaded that the producer's timetable was patently impossible, Selznick provided a spur. He spoke to composer Herbert Stothart about writing part of the score. When Steiner heard of this proposal through the musical grapevine, he quickened his pace and completed the music right on schedule.

Selznick directed Max Steiner to compose themes for each of the principal characters in the film. Thus, there was a theme for Scarlett, Rhett, Melanie, Gerald O'Hara, Bonnie, Mammy and Belle Watling—everyone in fact but Ashley, who being a gentleman would not have complained.

Hazel Rogers (left), chief of hairdressing, seeks a hair style in an album of daquerreotypes. With her is technical advisor Susan Myrick.

Selznick was dismayed that the costumes had the crisp, false, fresh look of the Wardrobe Department, instead of the somewhat worn look of actual clothing. He acknowledged this was a familiar flaw of made-in-Hollywood films, but he would have none of it. His costumes, he demanded, were to be properly aged.

Miss Rogers applies her findings to Olivia de Havilland's hairdo.

PRODUCER
David O. Selznick

PUBLICITY	PHOTOGRAPHY	FILM EDITOR
Russell Birdwell	Ernest Haller Lee Garmes	Hal Kern

STILL PHOTOGRAPHER Fred Parrish	TECHNICOLOR CO. SUPERVISION Natalie Kalmus	TECHNICOLOR ASSOCIATES Ray Rennahan Wilfred Cline	SPECIAL PHOTOGRAPHIC EFFECTS Jack Cosgrove	ASSOCIATE FILM EDITOR James Newcom
	ASSOCIATE Henry Jaffa	CAMERA OPERATORS Arthur Arling Vincent Farrar		ASSISTANT FILM EDITORS Richard Van Enger Ernest Leadley

The ever meticulous Selznick was not happy with the color values of the film and replaced Lee Garmes with Ernest Haller as cinematographer. Despite midstream changes in cameraman, director, writers and others, the film retains an amazing visual unity, thanks to the scrupulous control of its producer, David Selznick.

Film editor Hal Kern examines part of the 160,000 feet of printed film.

The hours of film trimmed from Gone With the Wind *are no longer in existence so it is impossible to know if a baby or two was thrown out with the bath water. One might consult the original shooting script, if it existed. Members of the cast never received a complete script during production, only individual scenes. These were later withdrawn by the producer. The only complete script extant was prepared from the finished film and reflects it word for word and shot for shot.*

Hal Kern and editing crew.

Selznick plunged into the massive task of editing the final film. With his scurrying film editors and production assistants beside him, Selznick supervised editing sessions that ran two days and two nights without pause. Then, after a brief hiatus, they would launch into another sleepless period. Selznick's task was formidable: to trim thirty hours of film to four.

Walter Eggers and Allan Jackson of MGM Laboratories look on as cinematographer Ernest Haller makes an adjustment.

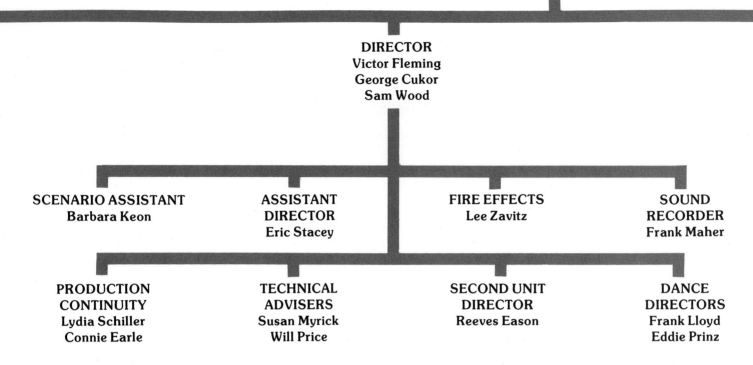

PRODUCER
David O. Selznick

DIRECTOR
Victor Fleming
George Cukor
Sam Wood

SCENARIO ASSISTANT
Barbara Keon

ASSISTANT DIRECTOR
Eric Stacey

FIRE EFFECTS
Lee Zavitz

SOUND RECORDER
Frank Maher

PRODUCTION CONTINUITY
Lydia Schiller
Connie Earle

TECHNICAL ADVISERS
Susan Myrick
Will Price

SECOND UNIT DIRECTOR
Reeves Eason

DANCE DIRECTORS
Frank Lloyd
Eddie Prinz

Selznick usually permitted his directors to direct. But sensing that GWTW was to be the high point of his career, this time he tried to turn his directors into mere extensions of himself. When Cukor protested, he was dismissed. When Fleming feigned a breakdown, he was replaced. And when Fleming recovered, his replacement remained.

Victor Fleming

George Cukor

Natalie Kalmus' husband was the inventor of the Technicolor process. As a byproduct of this relationship, Mrs. Kalmus was paid $1,000 a week for her advisory services on GWTW. She had the authority to scuttle any piece of wardrobe or set dressing that she judged would photograph badly. She created turmoil by tossing out entire sets, as Selznick's designers burned.

Margaret Mitchell urged Selznick to employ Susan Myrick to double-check his cast members' Southern dialects. Miss Myrick had another important virtue, said Miss Mitchell. "She knows all about Negroes and loves and understands them."

For the burning of Atlanta, Selznick's production crew threaded an intricate network of pipes through the facades of the buildings. Through the pipes, oil would be fed to fuel the great Atlanta fire. The Culver City Fire Department would be standing nervously by, ready to shoot down the soaring flames should they reach too high.

The burning of Atlanta.

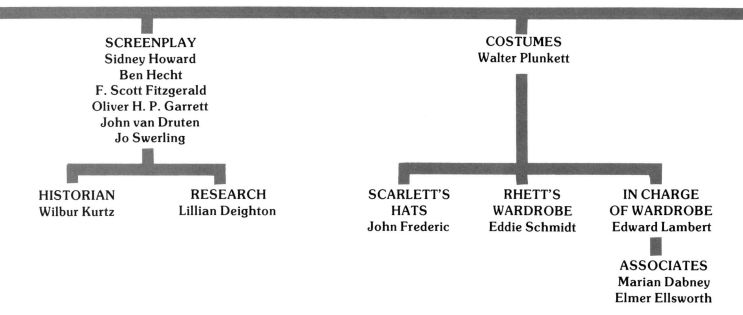

SCREENPLAY
Sidney Howard
Ben Hecht
F. Scott Fitzgerald
Oliver H. P. Garrett
John van Druten
Jo Swerling

COSTUMES
Walter Plunkett

HISTORIAN
Wilbur Kurtz

RESEARCH
Lillian Deighton

SCARLETT'S HATS
John Frederic

RHETT'S WARDROBE
Eddie Schmidt

IN CHARGE OF WARDROBE
Edward Lambert

ASSOCIATES
Marian Dabney
Elmer Ellsworth

The obsessive Selznick had a team of aides construct a complex breakdown of the novel that would have done credit to a computer expert. It consisted of a series of charts, tables and lists classifying all the principals of the novel, where they appeared, what they talked about, what they wore, their opinion of one another, etc. Selznick's aim was to trim redundancies from the script and avoid omitting anything of value.

Ben Hecht

F. Scott Fitzgerald

Scarlett wears the same humble cotton dress for over an hour of the film. Selznick ordered his seamstresses to make two dozen duplicates of the garment. The dresses were aged and treated to produce varying degrees of deterioration. Symbolists would say that the cotton dress reflected the onrushing decline of the Old South.

Selznick's Wardrobe Department fashions one of the 2,500 costumes worn by women in the film.

Selznick sent Walter Plunkett to Atlanta to discuss the coloration of Scarlett's costumes with Margaret Mitchell. Plunkett was also instructed to obtain samples of the cloth from circa 1860 dresses that reposed in local museums. Plunkett dispatched these fabrics to a waiting cotton mill in the North, which had contracted to provide Selznick with the bolts of cloth his seamstresses would need. The cotton mill would be well rewarded—it would be licensed to loom the only authorized "Gone With the Wind Cottons."

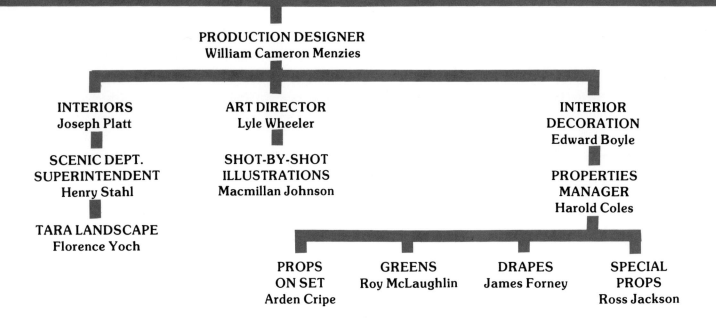

PRODUCER
David O. Selznick

PRODUCTION DESIGNER
William Cameron Menzies

INTERIORS
Joseph Platt

SCENIC DEPT.
SUPERINTENDENT
Henry Stahl

TARA LANDSCAPE
Florence Yoch

ART DIRECTOR
Lyle Wheeler

SHOT-BY-SHOT
ILLUSTRATIONS
Macmillan Johnson

INTERIOR
DECORATION
Edward Boyle

PROPERTIES
MANAGER
Harold Coles

PROPS
ON SET
Arden Cripe

GREENS
Roy McLaughlin

DRAPES
James Forney

SPECIAL
PROPS
Ross Jackson

Plunkett had the interesting job of designing an entire wardrobe for an actress who had not yet been selected. Blissfully unaware of her size, height, girth and coloring, Plunkett had to create a flattering array of costumes, from elegant to tacky, for this phantom actress.

Though Selznick hired and fired a parade of writers, including some of the greatest playwrights and novelists of our time, the completed script was primarily his own. It is impossible to compare what was jettisoned with what was retained, as Selznick was careful to suppress the original work and its many sets of changes, while releasing only the final script.

Tara was the key for Selznick in capturing the novel's charm. So not surprisingly he turned down the first twenty-five sketches of Tara that William Cameron Menzies submitted. Finally the frustrated designer disinterred the original drawing he had proposed, marked it "Proposal No. 26" and presented it to the producer. "Now you've got it," said Selznick. "That's Tara!"

A squad of illustrators churned out thousands of miniature color drawings of every shot as a guide and control for the director and cameraman. Thus, in a sense, the movie was "shot" before a single camera rolled. The only studio that exercises such pre-production control today is the Walt Disney Studios.

Joe Platt communicated with sources of antiques in every corner of the country. He purchased antiques with the profligacy of Citizen Kane stocking Xanadu. Selznick demanded verisimilitude in the interior decor of Tara and Twelve Oaks and ordered that antiques be put through an "aging" process.

Scarlett standing in front of the mantle at Tara.

CASTING MANAGERS
Charles Richards
Fred Schuesslee

| **TALENT SCOUT SOUTH** Max Arnow | **TALENT SCOUT NORTH & EAST** Oscar Serlin | **TALENT SCOUT WEST** Charles Morrison |

Selznick complained that the costumes on Gable's double were not creased in the same places as the star's. Some thought this excessively punctilious, but not Selznick. He feared these discrepancies would force him to eliminate some shots of the double in editing. Selznick ordered that someone be given sole authority for matching the creases in Gable's costumes with those of his double.

Selznick was aware of how certain types of fabric would photograph in the Technicolor process, and insisted on examining samples of every piece of cloth used in the film before the seamstresses did their work.

With uncharacteristic modesty, Selznick deferred to director Cukor in the matter of set decoration. He felt that Cukor had superior instincts in these matters and left to him the selection of the set decorator who would be choosing everything from drapes to end tables.

Cukor testing hopefuls for the roles of Melanie and Belle Watling.

Despite the cynical aims of the talent search for an unknown Scarlett, Selznick insisted on personally examining every foot of every screen test of these anonymous young women. He chafed at the task, feeling it an abysmal waste of time, but he screened them nonetheless.

Selznick fumed in marathon memos about Gable's costumes. They made the elegant Rhett Butler look as if he had bought his clothes off the rack, said Selznick. The look was especially egregious at the neckline where the collars hugged Gable so tightly that he looked grossly overweight.

113

TOIL
AND
TROUBLE

From the day that Gone With the Wind *went into production on January 26, 1939, it brought torment and turmoil into the lives of all the people who helped to create it.*

VIVIEN LEIGH: TORMENT.

George Cukor was the one ingredient that made Hollywood bearable to Vivien Leigh. And so it came as a cruel blow when, a scant two weeks into production, Cukor was dismissed. He had objected once too often to the producer's "improvements" in the Sidney Howard screenplay. To Vivien, Cukor's successor Victor Fleming seemed a mere technician. He was Gable's drinking buddy and seemed impatient with the nuances of character that Vivien sought to bring to the film.

The sound stage became a turbulent battleground between star and director. Vivien spoke her mind loudly and more often than even established stars are supposed to do. She had her own vision of the role of Scarlett, one she had molded with Cukor, and she would not retreat from it. Just how much of Gone With the Wind's *success is due to the stubbornness of Vivien Leigh and how much to the direction of Victor Fleming is a matter of conjecture.*

The appeal of Scarlett to millions of female readers rests in her fiery manner. Scarlett seems to be saying: "I will not be led by men. I will be the hammer, not the anvil." Vivien Leigh was also such a woman. She fought a continuing battle with her producer and director, both strong-minded men, and won as often as she lost.

She complained bitterly about Selznick's rewrites of playwright Sidney Howard's work until the producer finally brought the playwright to California to rework the

Vivien Leigh gives her lines a last once-over before the cameras start to roll.

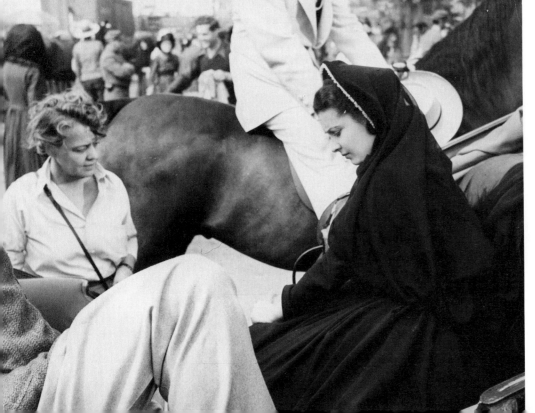

script. She would not accept Fleming's simplistic view that women are either good or bad and Scarlett was bad. There was a vulnerable side to Scarlett and she meant to show it. There was justification for Scarlett and she meant to examine it. Indeed, if Scarlett O'Hara were portrayed as nothing more than a scheming vixen, she would have joined an army of such characters who have been played by everyone from Bette Davis to Faye Dunaway and drifted off into oblivion, instead of becoming something of a legend.

Icy acrimony continued between Vivien Leigh and her director. Working under what she viewed as Fleming's horny-handed control, Vivien was anxious for the film to end. This attitude was extremely helpful to Fleming and he made the most of it. Vivien was worked long hours on the most lengthy schedule an actress ever endured. This frenzy crept into the character of Scarlett. Vivien's performance was further enhanced by her ardor for Olivier. Another actress might have been dazzled by the Gable charisma, but Vivien was too much in love with Olivier to be affected by it. This let her portray a Scarlett who was immune to the Butler charm.

The grueling days wore on. Five months of working six-day weeks would wear away a person of immense stamina. What it did to a woman with a dormant tubercular condition can only be imagined. The lack of sleep, the nervous exhaustion, the ubiquitous cigarettes were surely taking their toll.

The long days ground on, with Vivien working eighteen hours a day with rarely a day off. Then finally it drew to an end. Selznick summoned the actress to his office. She had endured a shooting schedule that no actress had ever faced before, with a director she despised, a script she deplored. She had survived on about three hours sleep a night for an extended period. When she entered Selznick's office after the final day of shooting, the producer looked up from a script he was reading and stared at the face of Vivien Leigh.

"My God," said Selznick with surprise, "you look old."

CLARK GABLE: TENSION.

Gable was always a suspicious man. On various occasions he felt that his producer and director were plotting to undermine his career. They would betray him or embarrass him before the camera, thought the King. In the atmosphere of the omnipotent studio, for a star who had come far and fast, such an attitude was not as neurotic as it might seem. As Henry Kissinger has observed, "Even a paranoic has his enemies." It is probable that George Cukor viewed Gone With the Wind as the story of Scarlett O'Hara and found the wise-cracking Rhett less essential to the texture of the film than the feisty Scarlett.

Gable felt himself put upon at every turn. The costume designer who had worked for him on all his previous films was denied to him. It was not until Selznick observed Gable's ill-fitting wardrobe in dailies that he dispatched one of his more volcanic memos, ordering that Gable's man be hired immediately!

Though Vivien Leigh was a relative newcomer to Hollywood, she seemed to sense Gable's uncertainty about the role and the director and tried to reassure him. These reassurances were no longer necessary when Selznick and Cukor quarreled and the director was replaced by Gable's friend Victor Fleming.

But even with Fleming, who was supportive and reassuring, the King continued to have his troubles. Gable was required to play a scene where, learning of Scarlett's miscarriage, he bursts into tears. Gable refused. Fleming managed the situation with a device that most actors today would find transparently fraudulent. He proposed that

Clark Gable walks toward the camera while rehearsing the Atlanta Bazaar scene.

they shoot the scene both ways. Selznick ended up using the version he wanted—with Gable crying.

Gable's problems did not end with his alienation from director Cukor, his antagonism toward producer Selznick, and his suspicions of the studio head who had sold him into bondage. Gable found Vivien Leigh chilly and aloof.

Shooting the film was as difficult as Gable had anticipated. Working at Selznick International after years in the MGM cocoon, Gable was a stranger on an unfamiliar lot. In addition, during the first half of the film, the activities of Vivien Leigh forced her into the spotlight. Gable found himself fighting to maintain his share of the story. It is a tribute to Gable's charisma that one never thinks of Leigh and Gable as anything but costars—though she worked twice as many days on the film as he did.

LESLIE HOWARD: DISSENSION.

As the filming of Gone With the Wind began, Leslie Howard found it as oppressive an experience as he had ever endured. He was not beautiful, he was not young, and he hated the herculean efforts of the makeup man to make him appear to be both. Scarlett's lust for Ashley Wilkes could only be made faintly credible if Ashley looked attractive, and so the hapless makeup man labored on, as Leslie Howard gritted his teeth.

As the shooting of GWTW stretched interminably and the filming of Intermezzo began elsewhere on the Selznick lot, Leslie Howard saw that his motive for playing the detested role of Ashley was built on sand. He would not be the associate producer of Intermezzo as he had been promised; he would merely play one more character in the chain of watery intellectuals who dotted his resumé. From the day he realized that his hopes of producing Intermezzo were a delusion, Leslie Howard began to show up late on the set of Gone With the Wind. He seldom studied his scenes. Numberless takes had to be reshot. As the producing bait vanished, the incentive deteriorated. Leslie Howard saw himself trapped once more in a role he abhorred.

He could not escape from Hollywood typecasting. It would have given him scant comfort to know that in the years ahead, neither Clark Gable nor Vivien Leigh would escape from their typecasting either.

OLIVIA DE HAVILLAND: REBELLION.

Olivia de Havilland stood ready to sacrifice everything, even beauty, for the sake of the role of Melanie. When director George Cukor offered her the choice of two

Leslie Howard inspects one of the cameras.

hair styles, she promptly chose the less attractive one because it was more true to the period.

Olivia's gentleman friend at the time took one look at the hairdo and balked. Her beauty had been compromised. Olivia's friend was a solemn young man of thirty-three who admired her devotion to her work and doubtlessly saw in it a reflection of his own steel-trap mind. He had dreams of a future in moviemaking and aeronautics. His name was Howard Hughes.

When Cukor was dismissed and Fleming took up the reins, Olivia joined Vivien Leigh in a frontal assault on the office of producer Selznick. The two women attacked him with logic, persuasion and hysteria in an effort to get him to reinstate the director they trusted. All to no avail.

Olivia was depressed at the insensitivity of Cukor's replacement, and in moments of doubt she would steal over to Cukor's home and ask his advice on how to play an upcoming scene. On one of these occasions, Cukor listened while Olivia ventilated her doubts, then led her to a sound decision. As she was leaving, Olivia expressed a feeling of guilt that, unknown to her fellow performers, she was coming to Cukor's house on Sundays to seek his help. Cukor replied that her guilt feelings were uncalled for. "After all," he said, "Vivien is coming to see me on Saturdays."

DAVID O. SELZNICK: TURMOIL.

As Gone With the Wind began production, Selznick sensed that this was not "just another epic." The daily rushes told him that here was a classic in the making, one that would bring him fame and immortality. This belief led him to intensify his own attention to every phase of production. In the past, David Selznick had been a punctilious producer; now he became an obsessed one.

Selznick had never undertaken such a massive project before, and the jackals of Hollywood were mocking his project as "the biggest bust in town," an

David O. Selznick

118

appellation heretofore reserved for Mae West. Selznick thus felt that Gone With the Wind demanded even more of him than his customary passion for details. As the film continued its relentless shooting schedule, Selznick insisted on personally approving every aspect of the production. This led to lengthy delays which in turn sharply increased the cost of production and drove him back to the bankers for further financing. Selznick had the dedicated frenzy of the true creator: damn the cost, the film's the thing. This attitude has sometimes produced moneymakers, but it has also produced its share of disasters. To Selznick's credit, he never doubted that he was mining pure gold.

Selznick's obsession with Gone With the Wind took its toll on the nerves of actors, directors and secretaries alike. But it also took its toll on the producer himself. He became more petulant and thoughtless of his staff. The ubiquitous memos multiplied and rained down upon the entire company.

At a certain point, Selznick began to doubt the results of all his efforts. Everything seemed to displease him. He would screen rushes over and over, declaring irritably that Tara looked all wrong, that Scarlett's dresses looked too new, that the Technicolor process was not rendering his sets properly, that the

Southern accents did not sound authentic.

But Selznick's fears were unfounded. The final film showed the values that he had lavished upon it. He had assembled a singular cast, marshaled an army of artists to create their surroundings, and sculpted a series of riveting scenes. He had every right to the triumphant film that his passionate attention and stubborn courage had produced.

GEORGE CUKOR: USURPATION.

The chief victim of David Selznick's belief that Gone With the Wind would establish his place in screen history was George Cukor. The director had worked amicably with Selznick on several films in the past. But Selznick's obsession with GWTW was such that he now usurped the director's job of directing.

Selznick became a producer-director-writer, and his hyphenated intrusions became intolerable to Cukor Now he demanded to see each major scene rehearsed. It was a situation to which an amiable hack might adjust, but Cukor could not.

George Cukor also suffered from Clark Gable's sense of insecurity. Gable was never comfortable in the role in which the American public had cast him, and now he found himself in the hands of

a so-called "woman's director," who would undoubtedly, thought Gable, throw the film to the ladies. Cukor sensed a widening gulf between himself and the star.

The director's time was running out. The end for Cukor came two weeks into production, as Selznick was viewing the previous day's rushes. Cukor had been under orders not to add any of his own dialogue to the scenes. Suddenly the producer froze. Up on the screen, Olivia de Havilland was delivering an impassioned speech in the Atlanta Bazaar Scene. The dialogue was nowhere in the script. Cukor had written it on the set and inserted it in the film. Selznick summoned the director. Cukor's defense was that Selznick's eleventh hour rewrite was unplayable. Selznick's response was that Cukor must go.

And so, nineteen days into production and two-and-a-half years after his labors had begun, George Cukor was dismissed.

VICTOR FLEMING: BREAKDOWN.

Gable finally had a "man's director." He did nothing to conceal his joy and Fleming did nothing to conceal his camaraderie with Gable, to the dismay of his female stars, who felt themselves abandoned.

Fleming did not accept the assignment with any great

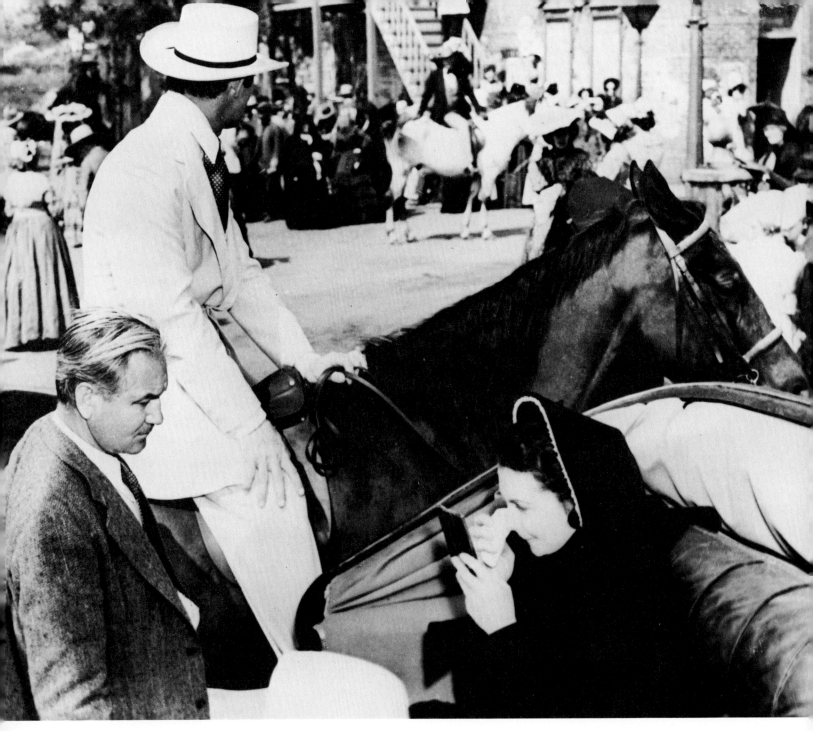

Victor Fleming with Vivien Leigh

relish. For one thing, he subscribed to the industry view that Gone With the Wind was a disaster in the making. Furthermore, he found the script, in his inelegant assessment, "no fucking good."

When production resumed, Fleming announced to a startled company that he had a new vision of Gone With the Wind. "I'm going to make it a melodrama," he declared. This must have given pause to Vivien Leigh and Olivia de Havilland, who could see all the intimate qualities of the film buried in the propwash of Test Pilot.

Fleming's formula was to browbeat cast and crew into compliance — excepting Gable, of course. The tough guy had replaced the aesthete. The man who had flown airplanes in World War I, hunted tigers in India, and taken racing cars through hairpin turns was pushing Gone With the Wind forward like a drill sergeant pushing his recruits on a forced march. One scene followed another, as the virile Fleming picked up the pace. While he stroked Gable, he reserved his petulance for Vivien Leigh.

120

Within a month, there was a fresh crisis. Fleming was suffering from physical and mental exhaustion. After a noisy altercation with Vivien Leigh, Fleming threw down the script, marched off the set and drove off the lot. He closeted himself in his home, inaccessible to phone calls and entreaties. Callers were told the director had suffered a nervous collapse. Fleming's physical stamina and emotional balance were indeed overtaxed, but the nervous collapse was feigned. It was a protest against Selznick's interference and Vivien Leigh's complaints.

Selznick was not to be finessed by this ersatz breakdown. Feeling that the best way to bring Fleming to heel was to replace him, Selznick contacted Sam Wood, who had just completed the filming of Goodbye, Mr. Chips, and hired him to replace Fleming.

Selznick's gambit proved effective. A bare fortnight later, Fleming "recovered." But Selznick wanted to give Fleming a clear signal that he was not indispensable. So when Victor Fleming returned, Sam Wood remained. Both directors continued working in tandem on alternating scenes. This placed the actors in the schizophrenic position of being directed by one man in the morning and another in the afternoon. There is no better way to cow a subordinate than to have another man performing his tasks. It is not perhaps the best means of encouraging creativity, but at this point Selznick was more concerned with obedience. He wanted two faithful surrogates, not one inspired innovator.

Fleming could not have foreseen that Gone With the Wind would become his most prestigious credit. His lack of foresight cost him dearly. Selznick offered to give Fleming a percentage of the movie's profits if he would waive a portion of his salary. Fleming shrugged the idea aside. "You must think I'm an idiot," he said. "This movie is going to be the biggest white elephant of all time."

SAM WOOD: CARPENTRY.

When Sam Wood flew back from England where he had been filming Goodbye, Mr. Chips, he was scarcely prepared for the long distance phone call from David Selznick, informing him that Victor Fleming had collapsed and beckoning him to a place in immortality. Sam Wood took up the reins.

Wood had only one shortcoming as a director: an almost total lack of imagination. After the aesthete and the adventurer, Selznick had called in the carpenter. He had no visual perception, which might be thought a major flaw in the director of such a rich canvas as Gone With the Wind. But Sam Wood had the support of the most brilliant art director that Hollywood had ever produced, William Cameron Menzies. Indeed, it was this association which enriched his career in later years, when he worked with Menzies on several distinguished films.

As Sam Wood resumed shooting on Gone With the Wind, once more Gable, Leigh, Howard and de Havilland were forced to adjust to a different drummer. Fortunately for posterity, the performers by now had been well grounded in their characters and were virtually director-proof.

Wood's most recent assignments at MGM prior to Goodbye, Mr. Chips were the two Marx Brothers farragos, A Day at the Races and A Night at the Opera. Whatever affection that lovers of the madcap brothers may feel for these zany epics, they do not seem to provide the proper credentials for the director of Gone With the Wind. But no doubt the very limitations in Sam Wood's creative gifts made him appealing to Selznick at this stage in the production. He wanted a conduit, not a creator.

Sam Wood directed over thirty minutes of Gone With the Wind, but expressed no particular displeasure when he was informed that he would not share in the screen credits for the film

THE WAR AND THE WIND

In 1938 David Selznick was in the midst of a campaign to discover a Scarlett O'Hara for Gone With the Wind.

In 1938 Adolf Hitler was in the midst of a campaign to conquer Europe.

In isolationist America, the Selznick campaign was infinitely more interesting than Hitler's.

1938

THE WIND	THE WAR
Jan. 30 Selznick shelves Sidney Howard's screenplay when playwright refuses further rewriting.	Austrian police discover plans for counterfeit revolt to justify invasion by German army.
Feb. 5 Historian Wilbur Kurtz leaves for Hollywood to work as technical adviser on GWTW.	Franz von Papen meets with Hitler at Berchtesgaden and learns of generals' opposition.
Feb. 12 Paulette Goddard is prepared to test for the role of Scarlett.	Hitler delivers ultimatum to Austrian chancellor to turn over his government to Nazis within the week.
Feb. 14 Wire service mistakenly reports that Paulette Goddard has been cast as Scarlett.	Austria delays and Hitler makes military preparations.
Feb. 15 Margaret Mitchell's novel goes into its forty-first printing.	In the face of threat of armed invasion, Austria gives in to German demands.
Feb. 20 Walter Plunkett completes costume designs and leaves on European vacation.	Massive Nazi demonstrations erupt throughout Austria.
Feb. 24 William Cameron Menzies completes 100 watercolor sketches to help budget film.	Austrian chancellor declares that his country will make no further concessions to Germany.
Mar. 3 GWTW finally falls off the bestseller list.	One hundred German officers summoned to see Hitler about Austrian invasion.

Mar. 9	Hal Kern is hired as film editor.	Austrian chancellor orders a plebiscite, sending Hitler into a fury.
Mar. 10	Will Price is hired as Southern dialogue coach for screen tests.	Ribbentrop reports to Hitler that England would do nothing if Austria were invaded.
Mar. 14	Selznick's research department starts indexing props needed from the novel.	Hitler makes his triumphal entry into Vienna.
Apr. 10	RKO volunteers Joan Fontaine for Melanie role, she suggests her sister Olivia.	Vienna Nazis unleash orgy of sadism against Jews, force them to scrub gutters before jeering Storm Troopers.
Apr. 13	Lucille Ball reads for role of Scarlett, Selznick is unimpressed.	Tens of thousands of Jews jailed, their worldly possessions confiscated.
Apr. 15	Designer Hattie Carnegie advertises a new gown inspired by Scarlett O'Hara.	Agency formed to permit Jews to buy their way out of country, headed by Adolf Eichmann.
Apr. 20	Women's Wear Daily suggests that dress shops use "Scarlett green" as promotional device.	Himmler sets up concentration camp in Mauthausen, Austria.
Apr. 21	Manhattan interior decorator requests permission to sell GWTW wallpaper.	German businessmen pour into Austria to buy up companies of dispossessed Jews.
Apr. 25	Gone With the Wind is published in Czechoslovakia.	Hitler summons General Keitel to plan the destruction of Czechoslovakia.

May 7	Margaret Mitchell learns that GWTW has earned an additional $90,000 in royalties.	Britain and France urge Czech government to meet Hitler's demands for Sudetenland.
May 14	Scarlett O'Hara bonnets go on sale at millinery shops.	U.S. ambassador to Germany is told that Czechs are provoking a crisis.
May 16	Bonwit Teller's advertises Civil War Southern belle fashions.	Hitler asks how many German divisions are available for immediate invasion of Czechoslovakia.

THE WIND	THE WAR
May 20 All American Seed Selection Society awards its gold medal to the Scarlett O'Hara Morning Glory.	Hitler's plans for Czech invasion leak out.
May 28 Press reports erroneously that Margaret Mitchell has gone to Hollywood to write sequel to Gone With the Wind.	Hitler addresses officers of Wehrmacht, orders preparation for military action against Czechs.
May 30 Selznick tries to loan Gary Cooper from Sam Goldwyn to play Rhett.	German generals oppose invasion of Czechoslovakia, fear Western powers' intervention.
June 18 Gable loan-out deal completed between Selznick and MGM.	Hitler issues order for action against Czechoslovakia on October 1.
July 19 Selznick suggests he might film GWTW in black and white.	Chief of German Army General Staff opposes Hitler's plans to invade Czechoslovakia, to no avail.
Aug. 26 Press is informed that Clark Gable has signed to play Rhett Butler.	Hitler tours the Western fortifications, launches construction of the West Wall.
Sept. 3 Screen Guide magazine announces that Norma Shearer and Clark Gable have won the leads in GWTW.	Hitler assembles his High Command, orders field units to move to Czech border.
Sept. 12 Selznick authorizes set construction and costume manufacture to begin.	Hitler addresses Nuremberg party rally, denounces Czechs to delirious mass of Nazis.
Sept. 13 Scribner's calls Margaret Mitchell one of the most overrated people in America.	French cabinet deadlocked on whether to honor its pledge to Czechs in case of German attack.
Sept. 15 Clare Boothe's comedy Kiss the Boys Goodbye opens on Broadway with Scarlett spoof.	Chamberlain goes to Berchtesgarden, agrees to Hitler's demands for the Sudetenland.
Sept. 18 Margaret Mitchell receives medal for most outstanding contribution to Southern literature.	British and French agree to Hitler's demands, present proposal to Czechs and advise speedy agreement.
Sept. 22 New York newspaper misquotes Margaret Mitchell as endorsing Katharine Hepburn for role of Scarlett O'Hara.	Hitler and Chamberlain meet again in Godesberg. Opposition growing in England to Chamberlain's policy of appeasement.
Sept. 28 Gone With the Wind is included in the time capsule buried at the World's Fair.	Goering tells Hitler: "A great war cannot be avoided any longer."

Sept. 29	Selznick receives production estimate of $2,250,000, asks for breakdown by scenes.	Chamberlain meets with Hitler and Mussolini at Munich, signs the Munich Pact.
Sept. 30	Selznick worries that Leslie Howard is too old for the role of Ashley.	Chamberlain returns to London, boasts of "peace in our time."
Oct. 21	Selznick asks Sidney Howard to join him in rewriting the script.	Hitler orders liquidation of remainder of Czechoslovakia.
Nov. 9	Selznick upbraids his casting department for its inadequate efforts.	Synagogues burned down, homes and shops of Jews destroyed and looted, night of horror throughout Germany.
Nov. 20	Selznick rules out Jeffrey Lynn as Ashley, vetoes Susan Hayward as Scarlett.	Czechoslovakia cedes Germany 11,000 square miles of its territory.
Dec. 6	Selznick notifies Katharine Hepburn, Jean Arthur, Joan Bennett and Loretta Young that they are the frontrunners.	Germany and France sign pact of friendship.
Dec. 25	Selznick suggests that Tallulah Bankhead play Belle Watling instead of Scarlett.	To please Hitler, the Czech cabinet suspends all Jewish schoolteachers.

1939

THE WIND

THE WAR

Jan. 11	Selznick notifies Margaret Mitchell of his choice of Vivien Leigh.	Chamberlain journeys to Rome to improve Anglo-Italian relations.
Jan. 26	George Cukor calls "action" as filming of GWTW begins.	Czech foreign minister states that the incorporation of Czechoslovakia into the Reich is imminent.

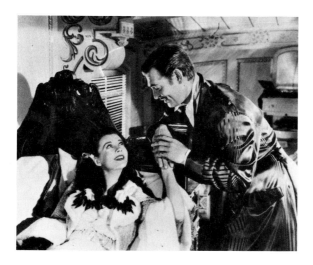

Feb. 13	George Cukor is dismissed.	British government asks Berlin to act on promises of the Munich agreement.

THE WIND

Feb. 15 Victor Fleming is hired and Ben Hecht begins to rewrite script.

Mar. 1 Shooting resumes with Fleming at the helm. He films the Atlanta Bazaar Scene.

Mar. 15 Selznick demands that costumes dramatize the decline of the South.

Mar. 17 Selznick unhappy with look of filming Tara on back lot.

Mar. 18 Vivien Leigh writes her husband: "It's miserable . . . I was a fool to do it."

Mar. 21 Selznick orders composer Max Steiner to study the music of the Civil War.

Mar. 22 Selznick finds filmed scenes are too dark.

Mar. 30 Selznick replaces cameraman Lee Garmes with Ernest Haller.

Apr. 1 Vivien Leigh is promised that Sidney Howard will return and work on script.

Apr. 3 Atlanta Exodus Scene is filmed.

Apr. 6 Gable returns from honeymoon with Carole Lombard.

Apr. 7 Selznick begins seeking replacement for Fleming.

Apr. 28 Selznick is furious because the costumes on Gable's stuntman aren't properly creased.

THE WAR

Hitler tells England he is not ready to act on his Munich guarantees.

Dr. Goebbels whips German press into a frenzy over invented acts of terror by the Czechs.

German troops pour into Czechoslovakia, meeting no resistance.

British cabinet opposes further appeasement of Hitler.

British and French governments make formal protests of German destruction of Czechoslovakia.

French propose that England, France, Russia and Poland join together to stop Hitler.

Hitler demands Danzig.

Reports appear of imminent German attack on Poland.

Hitler speaks at launching of battleship Tirpitz, rages over England's support of Poland.

Hitler issues secret plan for the destruction of Poland.

England signs agreement with Poland guaranteeing assistance in the event of attack.

Mussolini sends his troops into Albania.

Hitler ridicules Roosevelt, calling his concern "stupid imagination."

May 1	Sam Wood replaces Fleming.	Mussolini proposes military alliance to Hitler.
May 22	Famous crane shot is filmed of Confederate wounded, showing futility of war.	The Pact of Steel is signed, forming military alliance between Germany and Italy.

May 23	Gable carries Vivien Leigh upstairs in the famous Rape Scene.	Hitler tells his military chiefs that major war is inevitable.
May 27	Gable threatens to quit movie rather than cry.	Chamberlain explores mutual assistance pact with Russia.
May 30	Scene of Belle Watling on church steps is reshot at insistence of Hays Office.	Hitler approaches Moscow about possible Russo-German agreement.
June 10	Margaret Mitchell is awarded honorary degree at Smith College.	Russia asks English Foreign Secretary to come to Moscow and he refuses.
June 27	Filming of Gone With the Wind is completed.	Hitler receives plan for surprise invasion of Poland.
July 3	Vivien Leigh joins Laurence Olivier in New York.	Russia makes fresh initiative to Hitler.
July 11	Vivien Leigh and Laurence Oliver sail for England.	England finally agrees to hold staff talks with Russia.
July 18	Look magazine shows Vivien Leigh in her velvet costume.	Germany and Soviet Russia discuss pact.
Aug. 7	Selznick assures mayor of Atlanta that Gone With the Wind will be premiered there.	Hitler says he has reached the end of his patience with the Poles.
Aug. 14	Selznick enlists MGM support in releasing four-and-a-half-hour movie.	The annual Nuremberg Peace Rally is canceled.

THE WIND

Aug. 20 *Selznick weighs burning all photos of film to prevent premature publicity.*

Aug. 25 *Vivien Leigh does third retake of the porch scene.*

Sept. 2 *Leslie Howard returns to England.*

Sept. 8 *Vivien Leigh and Laurence Oliver relax on Ronald Colman's yacht.*

Sept. 28 *Selznick asks Ben Hecht to write seven title cards for the film.*

Oct. 7 *MGM demands that Gable's name be placed above the title.*

Oc. 12 *Selznick fights the Hays Office on "Frankly, my dear, I don't give a damn."*

Nov. 7 *Selznick demands daily reports on progress of musical score.*

Nov. 8 *Selznick orders one minute of overture before second half of GWTW.*

Nov. 25 *Selznick angry over paucity of publicity on GWTW.*

Dec. 15 *GWTW premieres in Atlanta. Mayor arranges triumphal motorcade.*

Dec. 25 *Selznick sends bound copy of script to cast and crew.*

THE WAR

Hitler signs German-Soviet nonaggression pact including plan for dividing up Poland.

German army begins invasion of Poland.

England and France inform Hitler that unless Germany withdraws its troops a state of war will exist. Hitler does not respond and World War II begins.

German panzer units reach Warsaw.

Russian army moves into stricken Poland.

Hitler appoints Himmler to head organization to annihilate Polish Jews.

Hitler calls for an attack on England and France as soon as possible.

Hitler prepares proclamation to the Dutch justifying his planned attack.

Bomb explodes in beerhouse in attempt on the fuehrer's life.

Hitler overcomes reluctance of his generals to widen the war.

Hitler postpones attack on the West till after new year. Christmas leaves are granted.

Hitler and Stalin exchange greetings.

THE OTHERS

David Selznick was obsessed with every detail of his films. He was as fastidious about draperies as about adverbs. But he was most fastidious of all about actors. He would often say that during the instant that a bit player is on the screen, he is the star of the film. During that moment the bit player occupies the total attention of the audience. Selznick felt it was folly to try to save money on small roles. The time that an inexperienced actor cost through the director's efforts lost more than the saving over actors of excellence. Therefore Selznick labored over the choice of every role in Gone With the Wind, and his care was repaid by a film of consummate quality.

CAREEN O'HARA.

For the role of Scarlett's youngest sister, Selznick ordered that Judy Garland be tested. But with Shirley Temple's rejection of the role of Dorothy in The Wizard of Oz, and Judy's acceptance of

the role, Miss Garland was beyond the scope of such a marginal role. Instead it was offered to the girl who played Andy Hardy's girlfriend in a dozen MGM films, Ann Rutherford.

SUELLEN O'HARA.

"I don't know anything about Evelyn Keyes and will be interested to see her," wrote Selznick. When he finally met the pretty actress from Atlanta, Selznick promptly chased her around his office until he finally

abandoned the pursuit in frustration and fatigue. Though Evelyn eluded the producer, to his credit he did not hold it against her. He

cast Evelyn Keyes as Suellen O'Hara without benefit of casting couch. Years later, when Evelyn Keyes wrote her memoirs, she called the book Scarlett O'Hara's Younger Sister. Ann Rutherford would have to find another title.

STUART TARLETON.

Selznick found George Reeves acting at the Pasadena Playhouse and

signed him to the highly visible role of Stuart Tarleton in the opening scene of Gone With the Wind. *The handsome young actor moved fast and far. After GWTW, Selznick sold Reeves' contract to Jack Warner. Following a few films at the Burbank studio, George Reeves marched off to war. Soon after his return, he was cast in another highly visible role — TV's Superman.*

PRISSY.
Selznick found the ideal actress to play the scatter-brained black maid. But

Butterfly McQueen was unwilling to be forever typecast in the role that had become an embarrassment to many of her race. After being cast as the stereotyped domestic in a handful of subsequent films, Miss McQueen determined she would never accept such a role again. Her agent so informed the press, and with that blow for freedom, her screen career slid into oblivion.

MRS. O'HARA.
Selznick was troubled about filling the role of Scarlett's mother — there were precious few contenders. He spoke to Lillian Gish and considered Cornelia Otis Skinner, before finally settling on Barbara O'Neil. Miss O'Neil, the one-time wife of director Joshua Logan, had shown the warm quality Selznick needed as the wife in Stella Dallas.

GERALD O'HARA.
Selznick had no other choice but Thomas Mitchell for the role of Scarlett's father. The warmhearted Irish actor was born for the role of the warmhearted Irish plantation owner. Selznick's options were so limited that the dogmatic negotiator was forced to bow to Mitchell's demand that he need never ride a horse in the film. This posed something of a problem in that Gerald O'Hara's sole obsession — besides the red earth of Tara — is horses.

MAMMY.
In casting the role of Mammy, Selznick did his work not wisely but too well. For in choosing Hattie McDaniel he established the quintessential Southern mammy who would forever be the focus of racist accusations about the film.

Whenever Miss McDaniel was reproached for playing the stereotypical domestic, she would point out the long periods when, lacking employment in films, she had to work as a real domestic. The screen work, she observed gently, was preferable. At a time when Hollywood and its audiences were ruled by sterotyped conceptions, Hattie McDaniel appeared again and again as a screen domestic — in Showboat, Saratoga, Song of the South and Selznick's own Since You Went Away.

DR. MEADE.
Selznick could choose from an embarrassment of riches in casting the role of the crotchety Dr. Meade. Lionel Barrymore was Selznick's first choice. "Get him," he snapped. But during the film's long gestation, Barrymore became confined to a wheelchair by a crippling arthritis. Selznick then

considered Andy Hardy's father, Lewis Stone, despite opposition in his own studio. He finally settled on the venerable Harry Davenport, who enjoyed the longest career of any of the Gone With the Wind cast — seventy-eight years.

AUNT PITTYPAT HAMILTON.
Billie Burke had beseeched Selznick for a chance to test for the role of Aunt Pittypat. Margaret Mitchell had described Scarlett's aunt as quaint and plump. So for her screen test, the trim Miss

Burke required pounds of padding in her gown as well as in her makeup. As her screen test proceeded and the oppressive lighting bore down on her burden of padding, Miss Burke nearly passed out from the heat. The test was a fiasco. Three days later Selznick signed Laura Hope Crews for the part.

FRANK KENNEDY.
Most of the actors in Gone With the Wind either came from a successful screen career or were launched on one. An exception was Carroll Nye. The spotlight eluded him throughout the thirties when he played a series of minor roles. The role of Scarlett's second husband, Frank Kennedy, seemed to promise a new beginning, but it never materialized. In the film, Frank Kennedy dies in a raid on Shanty Town, and Carroll Nye's movie career fared no better.

BELLE WATLING.
The Atlanta madam was a delicious and vexing role. Selznick thought of using Mae

West to play her "as a stunt." He considered Tallulah Bankhead for the part but was afraid to ask her. He weighed Joan Blondell and Loretta Young and found them wanting. Finally a musical-comedy star named Ona Munson tested for the role. She had toured in No, No, Nanette and played Lorelei Kilburn in radio's "Big Town." Her screen test was riveting, and Selznick knew at once that he had found his sympathetic madam.

CHARLES HAMILTON.

For the role of Scarlett's first husband, Selznick chose a young man he had first seen in an MGM film called Dramatic School. Melanie's ingenuous younger brother catches Scarlett on the rebound, marries her, and dies of measles at the front. Rand Brooks went on to a career as Hopalong Cassidy's sidekick in a series of Western movies. Victor Fleming cast him in the director's last project, the ponderous Joan of Arc. Rand Brooks married Stan Laurel's daughter and finally deserted the Hollywood scene.

MAYBELLE MERRIWETHER.

When Selznick sent George Cukor and Max Arnow south in search of an unknown Scarlett, he had little hope of finding anything more than a wealth of publicity. What he did find in Birmingham was Mary Anderson, whom he cast as Maybelle Merriwether. Most of Miss Anderson's work in the film would end on the cutting-room floor. But the publicity she received on her discovery, when she was being touted as a dark-horse Scarlett, helped launch her career. She went on to important roles in Lifeboat, Wilson and The Song of Bernadette.

INDIA WILKES.

On his Southern search for a truly Southern Scarlett, George Cukor was just going through the motions. Then one evening he attended a performance of Lady Windermere's Fan in Charleston. A young woman named Alicia Rhett was delivering Oscar Wilde's epigrams with style and elan. Cukor promptly shipped her off to New York for a screen test amid a shower of publicity. Selznick cast her as India Wilkes, Scarlett's perennial critic. Margaret Mitchell liked the actress for her name, but Hollywood studios had harsher standards and Alicia Rhett's career began and ended with Gone With the Wind.

THE COMING OUT

Like most of the events in the creation of Gone With the Wind, *the Atlanta premiere was a case of glamour distilled out of turmoil.*

With the completion of the filming, a number of submerged resentments bobbed to the surface. When MGM issued a press release stating that Gone With the Wind *had three directors who were "supervised" by David O. Selznick, Victor Fleming exploded. Only he had directed the film and he was under no one's supervision.*

Fleming found a sympathetic ear in his friend Clark Gable, who harbored his own resentments toward David Selznick.

Meanwhile, the opening to end all openings was being planned for Atlanta. First scheduled for November 15, the anniversary of the burning of Atlanta, and later postponed to December 15 by the delays of post-production, Metro's advance men had arranged for a triumphal event second only to Hitler's arrival in Vienna.

The governor of Georgia had declared the day a state holiday. The mayor of Atlanta had declared a three-day festival. The governors of five Southern states would descend on the Loew's Grand Theatre on Peachtree Street along with a score of Hollywood celebrities and Wall Street money men and their ladies.

But sharing Fleming's umbrage, Gable was having second thoughts about attending the Atlanta festivities. And what would a premiere of Gone With the Wind *be without Rhett Butler? It was unthinkable.*

Howard Strickling, Metro's promotion chief and Gable's confidant, prevailed on the King to reconsider. Gable would come to Atlanta, but he would not travel three thousand miles in the same plane with David Selznick. Fortunately, a newly formed carrier called American Airlines was seeking publicity, and hastened to make available a special plane to Gable and his bride. Victor

Fleming still declined to come. He chose to sulk while Atlanta reveled.

When the plane bearing Selznick, Olivia de Havilland, Vivien Leigh, and Laurence Olivier set down at Atlanta airport, the only other notable absentee was Leslie Howard. With Hitler on the march and Britain close to war, he chose to return to his native England as soon as shooting ended on the film. The shooting in Europe was just starting.

Selznick's plane, with Leigh, Olivier, de Havilland, and Myron and Irene Selznick aboard, had landed. These celebrities cooled their heels on the tarmac as the American Airlines plane carrying Mr. and Mrs. Gable circled leisurely in the blue Georgia sky. On the runway, a forty-piece band played the only song they knew, a brassy version of "Dixie." They played it again and again. Upon hearing the melody, Vivien Leigh turned to Olivier and said: "Isn't that nice —

The Loew's Grand Theater in Atlanta, 8:15 P.M., Friday, December ▶ 15, 1939, the world premiere of Gone With the Wind *is about to begin.*

Vivien Leigh is escorted to the Atlanta premiere by Laurence Olivier. Their respective spouses read of the event in the London Times.

Gable and Lombard, who attended the tumultuous Atlanta premiere, here are seen at the Los Angeles opening.

Olivia de Havilland arrives for the New York premiere on the arm of new film discovery, Jimmy Stewart.

Joan Crawford, one of the bevy of super-stars who coveted the Scarlett role, attends the L.A. premiere with Cesar Romero.

James Roosevelt, son of that man in the White House, attends the Hollywood premiere.

Ann Rutherford, who played one of Scarlett's younger sisters—the other was Evelyn Keyes—attends the New York opening.

The stars—Leigh, Gable, de Havilland—and producer Selznick, meet novelist Margaret Mitchell for the first time at the Atlanta premiere.

137

they're playing the song from the picture."

Finally the Gable plane touched down for an unhurried landing and the King and Carole Lombard presented themselves to the crowd, along with the other luminaries who had remained in seclusion, not wanting to upstage the monarch of the screen.

The airport crowd was massive, and hundreds of thousands lined the street along which their open cars carried the movie contingent into town.

The triumphal motorcade from Atlanta Municipal Air Field took them to the Georgian Terrace Hotel, past streets that were lined six deep with Atlantans, as the band played "Dixie" interminably. Mayor Hartsfield had urged the citizens of Atlanta to dig into their trunks and bedeck themselves in Civil War finery as the motorcade passed. So there was a seeming time warp as the Selznick party, in their contemporary clothes, moved down a street lined with citizens in 1860 finery.

Resentments smoldered beneath the smiling faces that Gable and Selznick turned to the crowds. With an eye on the European headlines and another on Gable's

sensitivity, Selznick had opposed the triumphal parade to the last. Gable would hate it, said Selznick. The parade was absurd. "The idea of a town receiving us as though we had just licked the Germans!" snapped the producer. He anticipated being greeted by a barrage of eggs hurled by an enraged citizenry. But both Selznick and Gable did board the open cars and no eggs were in evidence, only cheers and Southern war cries, unheard since the glory days of the Confederacy.

On December 15, 1939, Atlanta became a microcosm of the United States in its frenzied welcome of the Selznick party. It was a commercial and sentimental field day. The opportunities for profit were not lost on local merchants in the pre-Christmas season, and along the motorcade route dozens of tie-in products — from dolls to candies — were presented for sale.

As the procession of open cars moved slowly through the black sections of town, the celebrities encountered some ambivalent stares from a people who had been freed by a bloody war seventy-five years before but by 1939 had seen few of the fruits of freedom.

The premiere was a triumph. From the opening credits to Scarlett's closing vow, the audience that crammed the Loew's Grand Theatre cheered and wept its delight. Selznick had touched a deep feeling of anger and pride in his Southern audience that swept over it like Sherman's furies.

Four days later Gone With the Wind moved to its Manhattan premieres at the Astor and the Capital theatres. All the principals save Gable accompanied the film to another triumphal reception. Though the New York critics were not as uniformly ecstatic, they were extremely supportive.

A week later it was Los Angeles' turn to feel the Wind. The opening at the Fox Cathay Circle Theatre was attended by virtually every actor, artist and executive who had anything to do with Gone With the Wind, either by participation or by exclusion. It was said at the time, "If a bomb dropped on the Cathay Circle tonight, Zachary Scott would be the biggest star in Hollywood."

To Atlanta, to New York, to Los Angeles, and soon to every city in America and around the world, Gone With the Wind had come, been seen and conquered.

Gone With The Wind

The cover of the program given out at the Atlanta premiere.

From the program

DAVID O. SELZNICK'S
production of
MARGARET MITCHELL'S
Story of the Old South

GONE WITH THE WIND

IN TECHNICOLOR, *starring*

CLARK GABLE

as Rhett Butler

LESLIE
HOWARD · de HAVILLAND

OLIVIA

and presenting

VIVIEN LEIGH

as Scarlett O'Hara

A SELZNICK INTERNATIONAL PICTURE

Directed by VICTOR FLEMING

Screen Play by Sidney Howard

Music by Max Steiner

A Metro-Goldwyn-Mayer Release

THE PLAYERS
in the order of their appearance

AT TARA,
The O'Hara Plantation in Georgia:

BRENT TARLETON	FRED CRANE
STUART TARLETON	GEORGE REEVES
SCARLETT O'HARA	VIVIEN LEIGH
MAMMY	HATTIE McDANIEL
BIG SAM	EVERETT BROWN
ELIJAH	ZACK WILLIAMS
GERALD O'HARA	THOMAS MITCHELL
PORK	OSCAR POLK
ELLEN O'HARA	BARBARA O'NEIL
JONAS WILKERSON	VICTOR JORY
SUELLEN O'HARA	EVELYN KEYES
CARREEN O'HARA	ANN RUTHERFORD
PRISSY	BUTTERFLY McQUEEN

AT TWELVE OAKS,
The nearby Wilkes Plantation:

JOHN WILKES	HOWARD HICKMAN
INDIA WILKES	ALICIA RHETT
ASHLEY WILKES	LESLIE HOWARD
MELANIE HAMILTON	OLIVIA DE HAVILLAND
CHARLES HAMILTON	RAND BROOKS
FRANK KENNEDY	CARROLL NYE
CATHLEEN CALVERT	MARCELLA MARTIN
RHETT BUTLER	CLARK GABLE

AT THE BAZAAR IN ATLANTA:

AUNT "PITTYPAT" HAMILTON	LAURA HOPE CREWS
DOCTOR MEADE	HARRY DAVENPORT
MRS. MEADE	LEONA ROBERTS
MRS. MERRIWETHER	JANE DARWELL
RENE PICARD	ALBERT MORIN
MAYBELLE MERRIWETHER	MARY ANDERSON
FANNY ELSING	TERRY SHERO
OLD LEVI	WILLIAM McCLAIN

OUTSIDE THE EXAMINER OFFICE:

UNCLE PETER	EDDIE ANDERSON
PHIL MEADE	JACKIE MORAN

AT THE HOSPITAL:

REMINISCENT SOLDIER	CLIFF EDWARD
BELLE WATLING	ONA MUNSON
THE SERGEANT	ED CHANDLER
A WOUNDED SOLDIER IN PAIN	GEORGE HACKATHORNE
A CONVALESCENT SOLDIER	ROSCOE ATES
A DYING SOLDIER	JOHN ARLEDGE
AN AMPUTATION CASE	ERIC LINDEN

The complete credits as presented in the program.

DURING THE EVACUATION:

A COMMANDING OFFICER . . . . . . .TOM TYLER

DURING THE SIEGE:

A MOUNTED OFFICER . . . . WILLIAM BAKEWELL
THE BARTENDER . . . . LEE PHELPS

GEORGIA AFTER SHERMAN:

A YANKEE DESERTER . . . . PAUL HURST
THE CARPETBAGGER'S FRIEND . ERNEST WHITMAN
A RETURNING VETERAN . . . WILLIAM STELLING
A HUNGRY SOLDIER . . . . LOUIS JEAN HEYDT
EMMY SLATTERY . . . . ISABEL JEWELL

DURING RECONSTRUCTION:

THE YANKEE MAJOR . . . . . ROBERT ELLIOTT
HIS POKER-PLAYING CAPTAINS . GEORGE MEEKER
                                                WALLIS CLARK
THE CORPORAL . . . . IRVING BACON
A CARPETBAGGER ORATOR . . . ADRIAN MORRIS
JOHNNY GALLEGHER . . . . . J. M. KERRIGAN
A YANKEE BUSINESSMAN . . . OLIN HOWLAND
A RENEGADE . . . . YAKIMA CANUTT
HIS COMPANION . . . . . BLUE WASHINGTON
TOM, A YANKEE CAPTAIN . . . . . WARD BOND
BONNIE BLUE BUTLER . . . . . . CAMMIE KING
BEAU WILKES . . . . MICKEY KUHN
BONNIE'S NURSE . . . . LILLIAN KEMBLE COOPER

PRODUCED BY DAVID O. SELZNICK • DIRECTED BY VICTOR FLEMING
BASED ON MARGARET MITCHELL'S NOVEL "GONE WITH THE WIND"

SCREEN PLAY BY SIDNEY HOWARD

The Production Designed By . . . *William Cameron Menzies*	Assistant Director . . . . *Eric G. Stacey*
Art Direction By . . . . *Lyle Wheeler*	Second Assistant Director . . . . . . *Ridgeway Callow*
Photographed By . . . . *Ernest Haller, A.S.C.*	Production Continuity . . . . *Lydia Schiller*
Technicolor Associates . . . . . *Ray Rennahan, A.S.C.*	*Connie Earle*
Wilfrid M. Cline, A.S.C.	Mechanical Engineer . . . . *R. D. Musgrave*
Musical Score By . . . . *Max Steiner*	Construction Superintendent . . . . . *Harold Fenton*
Associate . . . . *Lou Forbes*	Chief Grip . . . . *Fred Williams*
Special Photographic Effects By . . . . . . *Jack Cosgrove*	In Charge of Wardrobe . . . . . *Edward P. Lambert*
Associate: (Fire Effects) . . . . *Lee Zavitz*	Associates . . . . *Marian Dabney*
Costumes Designed By . . . . *Walter Plunkett*	*Elmer Ellsworth*
Scarlett's Hats By . . . . *John Frederics*	Casting Managers . . . . *Charles Richards*
Interiors By . . . . *Joseph B. Platt*	*Fred Schuessler*
Interior Decoration By . . . . . . *Edward G. Boyle*	Location Manager . . . . *Mason Litson*
Supervising Film Editor . . . . *Hal C. Kern*	Scenic Department Superintendent . . . *Henry J. Stahl*
Associate Film Editor . . . . . . *James E. Newcom*	Electrical Superintendent . . . . *Wally Oettel*
Scenario Assistant . . . . *Barbara Keon*	Chief Electrician . . . . *James Potevin*
Recorder . . . . *Frank Maher*	Properties:
Makeup and Hair Styling . . . . . *Monty Westmore*	Manager . . . . *Harold Coles*
Associates . . . . *Hazel Rogers*	On the Set . . . . *Arden Cripe*
Ben Nye	Greens . . . . *Roy A. McLaughlin*
Dance Directors . . . . *Frank Floyd*	Drapes . . . . *James Forney*
Eddie Prinz	Special Properties Made By . . . . . *Ross B. Jackman*
Historian . . . . *Wilbur G. Kurtz*	Tara Landscaped By . . . . *Florence Yoch*
Technical Advisers . . . . *Susan Myrick*	Still Photographer . . . . *Fred Parrish*
Will Price	Camera Operators . . . . *Arthur Arling*
Research . . . . *Lillian K. Deighton*	*Vincent Farrar*
Production Manager . . . . *Raymond A. Klune*	Assistant Film Editors . . . . *Richard Van Enger*
Technicolor Co. Supervisor . . . . . . *Natalie Kalmus*	*Ernest Leadley*
Associate . . . . *Henri Jaffa*	

A GWTW collage that appeared in the program.

THE FAN MAGAZINES EXPLODE

"I doubted Vivien could really play Scarlett..."

"That reaction certainly shows I'm no casting director!"

VIVIEN LEIGH, RHETT BUTLER, AND I

TO begin with I'd like to state that despite what a lot of papers said there was never any feud between Vivien Leigh and me during the filming of "Gone with the Wind" or at any time thereafter.

Hollywood goes just as much to extremes when it comes to male and female stars cast together as it does on any other subject. Get a man and a woman in a picture together and you are immediately reported as either fighting or romancing. The fact that in eighty per cent of your pictures you have no emotion about the beautiful creature opposite you, other than an interest in her acting ability, is never printed. Yet that's the truth more often than not.

As for any possibility of Vivien Leigh's falling in love with me I knew that was out from our first glance. For never have I seen any girl more completely in love than that one is—with Laurence Olivier. It's as visible as a Neon sign that she can't think or talk of or dream about anything or anyone else on earth—except when she's on the set. When she's on the set, she's what a good actress should be. She's all business.

As for my falling in love with her, I'm sure that could have been plenty pleasant except that, added to her lack of interest in me, I didn't have any heart to give away, either. Mine was staked out to that Lombard girl who is mighty beautiful and brainy. Carole and I weren't married when Vivien and I first met, but we did marry while I was working on the picture and there's a story about our wedding that has never been told and which I'll get to presently.

I'll be truthful about it, however; I'll confess that the first time I saw her I doubted that Vivien could really play Scarlett. That reaction certainly shows I'm no casting director. But, accustomed to the more abandoned and superficial personalities of Hollywood girls, Vivien seemed too demure to me, at that first meeting, for the vivid, relentless Scarlett.

David Selznick introduced us to each other at a dinner party at his home. Vivien was wearing a very plain, tailored dress. She's much tinier in real life than she appears on the screen, and since she uses little make-up she has

a very young, unsophisticated air. Besides, she had all the fires banked that evening and that Olivier guy was her escort.

Now I know I should have stopped to consider all that. But having seen Vivien only in "A Yank at Oxford," in which she didn't have a lot to do, I just looked at her that first evening at David's and wondered if that keen-minded producer had gone haywire when he signed her.

I knew he hadn't the first day Vivien and I got on a set together. (David doesn't go haywire, anyway, which is another thing I should have thought about—but as a profound thinker I'm a good duck-hunter.) The best alibi I can offer for my thickheadedness is that my mind was preoccupied with *Rhett Butler*. He had me plenty worried, so worried that I didn't want to play him.

Don't think that was because I didn't realize what a fat part he was. *Rhett* is one of the greatest male characters ever created. I knew that. I'd read the entire book through six times, trying to get his moods. I've still got a copy in my dressing room and I still read it

From Screen Guide (1940)

In an article called "Vivien Leigh, Rhett Butler and I," written by Clark Gable and "told to" Ruth Waterbury, Gable seems to be providing an offguard look at the stars of GWTW when the cameras stopped.

With disarming frankness, Gable acknowledges the rumors of a feud between Vivien Leigh and himself, then blandly attributes this to Hollywood gossip. He adds that "in eighty percent of your pictures you have no emotion" about your co-star.

There is no mention of Vivien Leigh's misery with the script, the firing of the director, and his replacement by Gable's crony.

Gable says that he and Vivien were not in love, since she was enamored with Laurence Olivier and his heart was in the hands of Carole Lombard, which makes for a sweet if unsurprising revelation.

Unmentioned are the facts that the morality clause in Vivien's contract was invoked to force Olivier out of her house, and that Gable took the Rhett Butler role to get the money to free himself of his wife.

Gable piques one's interest when he says that his first sight of the demure Vivien Leigh made him doubt whether she could play the fiery Scarlett.

He does not tell of the occasion when Victor Fleming, in a fury of frustration, told her to shove her script "up your royal ass" and stormed from the set.

In short, the articles on Gone With the Wind were like a burlesque stripper — they revealed what was interesting while concealing what was fascinating.

From Screen Guide (1940)

BY CLARK GABLE
AS TOLD TO RUTH WATERBURY

Everyone else has had his say about what went on behind the scenes of "Gone with the Wind." Now the hero himself, in a startlingly frank story, tells the truth about the year's most exciting cinematic event

From Motion Picture (1939)

From Photoplay (1940)

THE BOX-OFFICE RIVALS

Considering the public acclaim that greeted Gone With the Wind *when it appeared in theatres around the country, one would have thought that it was without competition at the box office. Quite the opposite was true. Hollywood produced a startling number of exceptional films in 1939.*

It is interesting to review the rivals of Gone With the Wind *and to observe how many of them had links to Selznick's production. It is also interesting to recall that all these films were the products of major studios, while* Gone With the Wind, *the best remembered of them all, was the product of a marginal studio and one fastidious man.*

THE WIZARD OF OZ.

When Selznick fired George Cukor and Gable chose Victor Fleming as his replacement, the director was knee-deep in Munchkins. Fleming abandoned the direction of MGM's Wizard of

Oz to go to work for the Wizard of Culver City. Like Gone With the Wind, The Wizard of Oz *has been frequently re-released, its appeal evergreen.*

GUNGA DIN.

Ben Hecht had worked on the script of Gone With the Wind *for seven days, a timetable that compares*

favorably with the creation of the world. He and Charles MacArthur took somewhat longer to write this adventurous confection based on the famous poem by Rudyard Kipling. In addition to Cary Grant and Douglas Fairbanks, it starred Scarlett reject Joan Fontaine.

THE OLD MAID.

Two of the most prominent Scarlett castoffs, Bette Davis and Miriam Hopkins, co-starred in this Warner Bros. film. Like Gone With the Wind, *it was based on a Pulitzer Prize-winning work,* a play by Zoë Akins. The prolific Max Steiner provided the musical score, with not a trace of Southern anthems.

GOLDEN BOY.

As faithful as David Selznick was to the prose of Margaret Mitchell, equally faithful was director Reuben Mamoulian to the prose of Clifford Odets in his adaptation of the Broadway play. Golden Boy marked the debut of an appealing young actor named William Holden.

THE WOMEN.

On the heels of his dismissal from Gone With the Wind, George Cukor, "the woman's director," guided a cast of 135 women through this adaptation of the nasty, gossipy Broadway hit by Clare Boothe. No less than 5 of the 135 ladies had been in the running for the role of Scarlett — Norma Shearer, Joan Crawford, Paulette Goddard, Joan Fontaine and Rosalind Russell.

GOODBYE, MR. CHIPS.

Victor Fleming came to Tara from The Wizard of Oz, and Sam Wood proceeded there from Goodbye, Mr. Chips. Like the Margaret Mitchell work, the James Hilton novel about the English schoolmaster had a faithful following. And Robert Donat's performance won him the Academy Award that was denied to Clark Gable.

JESSE JAMES.

Fox used the Technicolor process in a purported biography of the famous outlaw, with Tyrone Power inevitably cast in the title role. Randolph Scott, whom Selznick had considered for

the role of Rhett Butler for fully thirty minutes, played a supporting part.

DRUMS ALONG THE MOHAWK.

Gone With the Wind made investments in historical fiction seem respectable and safe. Fox adapted Walter Edmonds' novel to the screen in Technicolor, with Henry Fonda and Claudette Colbert. Miss Colbert flew to the Atlanta premiere of GWTW. "Poor deluded Claudette," said Selznick, "is coming under the notion that she is going to have a good time!"

THE
70 MM.
SOLUTION

There is a theory, first propounded by the Volkswagen people, that less is more. This concept was brought to mind by the conversion by MGM of Gone With the Wind into a wide-screen 70mm. version.

In the fifties, faced by the threat of television, motion pictures decided to think big, presenting their films in Cinemascope, Vistavision and other Brobdingnagian forms. This also required the enlargement on re-release of such classics as Gone With the Wind.

Unfortunately, in converting a 35mm. image, which approximated a square, to 70mm., which resembled a sort of giant picture postcard, it was necessary to lop off a portion of the top and bottom of the picture.

This meant that the viewer lost the tops of heads, the bottom of legs, far-off mountains, carpets, chandeliers, the scope of crowds and other expendables.

It meant that the composition of every scene as visualized by David Selznick, as illustrated by William Cameron Menzies, as directed by Cukor, Fleming and Wood, as captured by cinematographers Garmes and Haller, would be sacrificed on the altar of size.

It is a tribute to the riveting appeal of the story and the stars that in 70mm. re-release Gone With the Wind continued to attract huge audiences. The advertising made an unalloyed virtue of the change, trumpeting the expanded scope of the film.

There is no denying that the film had an increased visual impact in this new dimension. Though the aesthetic arrangement of actors and scenes was violated by the spread to 70mm., there was an overpowering sweep to the new screen size.

A technical bonus was a stereophonic soundtrack that was added to the film. It amplified such incidental sound effects as the rustle of hoopskirts and the creak of wagon wheels. Unfortunately, these gratuitous sounds, coming from whichever part of the screen the skirts or wagons appeared, often obliterated vital bits of dialogue.

If some found the visual and aural changes aesthetically harmful, the majority of filmgoers found the new and bigger movie entertaining and even overwhelming. In re-release, the movie led Variety's list of box-office hits week after week.

Thus Gone With the Wind, whose length and scope had dwarfed other films of the thirties, now reached the size of a football field and dwarfed other movies in physical size as well.

The conversion of the original 35mm. print of GWTW to its attenuated 70mm. form.

This is the 70mm. version.

This is the original GWTW.

This is the original GWTW.

This is the 70mm. version.

This is the 70mm. version.

This is the original GWTW.

This is the original GWTW.

This is the 70mm. version.

"DON'T SELL THE STEAK, SELL THE SIZZLE"

That advertising axiom was much in evidence in the wide-screen re-release of Gone With the Wind.

The most elaborate Press Book imaginable was issued to exhibitors. It embraced every aspect of promotion and merchandising known to man.

The re-release of the most successful, most beloved film of our time could have been expected to contain its own built-in momentum, but the marketing men of the movie colony were determined to make certainty double sure. They outdid themselves in inundating the public with publicity and promotions galore.

MUSIC

FIRST OFFICIAL SOUND TRACK ALBUM

Heading the record parade of GONE WITH THE WIND music, MGM Records is releasing the first album to be taken directly from the sound track of GONE WITH THE WIND. The album consists of 13 selections in stereophonic sound from Max Steiner's memorable score and features this official 32 page illustrated souvenir program of color photographs and text. See the promotion checklist below and plan a strong campaign around this album.

1. **CONTACT** your local MGM distributor (See list) and make arrangements for a cooperative effort on setting up music store window displays and interior exhibits;

2. **PLAN** to furnish your leading disc jockeys with copies of the album;

3. **ARRANGE** for tie-in album give-aways;

4. **PLAY** the album in advance through your lobby public address system, and use the recording for auditorium music before and after your current feature attraction;

5. **GIVE** the album as a gift to every newspaper movie critic and music critic.

MGM RECORD DISTRIBUTORS

COLUMBIA RECORDS

Columbia Records has produced the striking three-wing store display (above) featuring the well-known Legacy Albums in conjunction with GONE WITH THE WIND. This will be their major promotion piece used for national distribution.

The highly-acclaimed Legacy Series from Columbia Records provides a natural tie-in to this exciting release of GONE WITH THE WIND through the music with two outstanding albums: THE UNION and THE CONFEDERACY. These deluxe book and record packages recapture the stirring era of GONE WITH THE WIND through the music, the pictures, the words, and the sounds of this historic period. THE UNION contains a record featuring the marches and songs of the time, an authentic Civil War cannon shot, Lincoln's Gettysburg Address, and more, plus a 60-page picture book with essays by celebrated historians like Bruce Catton, Allan Nevins, and Clifford Dowdey. And the companion volume, THE CONFEDERACY, includes a recording of General Lee's Farewell Address spoken by his cousin, Rev. Edmond Jennings Lee, as well as the authentic rebel yell, and marches and songs of the Confederates, along with a 52-page picture book with essays by Bruce Catton and Clifford Dowdey.

Another Columbia album—and another natural for GONE WITH THE WIND promotion—is Percy Faith's top selling album (depicted on this page) of great motion picture themes, featuring "Tara's Theme" as the title number.

The Columbia Records field promotion staff (listed below) will be eager to cooperate with you in setting up counter displays, window displays, record give-away contests and other promotional activities.

RCA VICTOR

In conjunction with the re-release of GONE WITH THE WIND, RCA Victor Records is re-issuing its album of music composed and conducted by Max Steiner. The score which took three months to write, $100,000 to record, is reputed to be the longest ever composed for a film. For promotional purposes, you can obtain copies of these albums from the RCA field staff below.

RCA VICTOR RECORD FIELDMEN

COLUMBIA RECORDS FIELD PROMOTION STAFF

SHEET MUSIC

THE REMICK MUSIC CORPORATION has published sheet music featuring "Tara's Theme" and "My Own True Love", both depicted on this page. It is also issuing accordion, choral, orchestral and organ arrangements of "Tara's Theme."

Contact all retail outlets and provide them with stills, posters and other accessories that will attract public attention to window and interior displays.

Also, take advantage of any opportunity to present sheet music to local orchestras in night clubs, hotels, ballrooms and radio and television stations for playing during your run of GONE WITH THE WIND.

MUSIC.

MGM's record division published a sound track album of the Max Steiner score . . . RCA Victor issued an album of music from the film composed and conducted by Steiner . . . Remick Music published sheet music of "Tara's Theme" for piano, accordion, organ, orchestra and choir . . . Columbia Records issued two albums, "The Union" and "The Confederacy," featuring marches, songs and sounds of the era, including "an authentic Civil War cannon shot."

EVENING GOWN PROMOTION

EVENING GOWNS

Lend authenticity to your GONE WITH THE WIND activities by utilizing the many elements that contribute to the charm of the "Old South". Arrangements have been made with the manufacturer of evening gowns. Your premiere will surely be enhanced by the presence of attractive models in the Romantic Era dresses shown on this page. You may purchase these dresses directly at the nominal cost of $28.00 each. This includes both the dress and hoop skirt. We recommend the following colors: Light Blue, Pink, Pale Yellow, and White. Sizes range from 3-17 Junior and 4-20 Misses. Deliveries will be made two weeks following receipt of your order.

All orders should be directed to:

MR. EARL BIGBEE
MIKE BENET FORMALS
P.O. Drawer 43 • Pittsburg, Texas 75686
Telephone: Area Code 214 UN 4-3648

LE #246—A garland of imported roses adorn the ine and apron front of skirt on this dress of acetate de soie with ruffled petticoat of nylon net.

STYLE #298—A tremendous sweep of peau de soie trimmed with huge roses that peek through the ruffled petticoat of the dress.

STYLE #208—A fabulous ball gown with the look of pure silk, in softly shirred rayon habutae—traditionally "Old South".

EVENING GOWNS.

A company in Pittsburg, Texas was licensed to manufacture Gone With the Wind *evening gowns with the charm of the Old South, at a cost of $28 each in pale blue, pink, yellow and white.*

BOOKS.

Macmillan published a hardbound edition, a quality paperback edition, a large-print edition . . . Pocket Books released a mass paperback edition . . . A company in Los Angeles published The "GWTW" Cook Book of Southern Recipes.

PROMOTION IDEAS.

Theatre owners were urged to use the following tactics to build action at the box office:
●—*Hire young men and women to wear T-shirts at ball games and beaches reading "Don't Miss GWTW" with the name of the theatre on the back.*

BOOKS

POCKET BOOK

The Pocket Book edition of GONE WITH THE WIND, which has sold over two million copies since 1958, has been issued again in conjunction with the release of the movie. Utilizing as cover art the full color painting from the film's advertising campaign, Pocket Books has mounted an elaborate promotional campaign that has already increased sales 500% over the past two years.

Here's what to do . . .

1. CONTACT your local Pocket Book distributor. Tell him about your playdate. Ask him to set up counter, rack and window displays for which you will provide heralds and stills.

2. ARRANGE to send copies of the book to press, radio and television personalities, heads of key organizations, top political figures and other public opinion builders.

The Macmillan Company has announced publication of a new two-volume, large print set of GONE WITH THE WIND for readers who find normal print difficult. This edition is now on sale in quality book stores everywhere across the country for $13.95. In addition, Macmillan also has a paperback which retails at $2.85, a regular hard cover which sells for $5.95 and a deluxe edition at $10.00. Macmillan's Trade Sales Force (listed below) has been alerted to work with MGM's Field Press Representatives in arranging special displays and tie-in theatre/bookstore promotions as well as distribution of GONE WITH THE WIND book marks which can be made locally.

THE MACMILLAN COMPANY

TRADE SALES DEPARTMENT,
866 Third Avenue
New York, New York 10022

DIRECTOR OF TRADE SALES	ASSISTANT DIRECTOR OF TRADE SALES
Arthur Stiles	William Donovan
41 Westwood Lane	83 So. Barrington Road
Kings Park, N. Y. 11754	Barrington, Ill. 60010
516 265 8868	312 DU 1 4063

PRODUCT SALES MANAGER	SALES PROMOTION MANAGER
Robert Gold	Barbara Heckethorn
157 East 72nd Street	27 East 92nd Street
New York, N. Y. 10021	New York, N. Y. 10028
212 YU 8 2809	212 AT 9 3157

RESEARCH MANAGER
Lou Brooks
85 Fourth Avenue
New York, N. Y. 10003
212 473 5169

REGIONAL SALES MANAGERS

REGION I	REGION II	REGION IV	REGION V
Joseph Fortin	Kenneth Marshall	Joseph Friedman	Harry Creek
P. O. Box 1608	9207 Mackinaw Drive	1011 Nameoke Street	2257 Beecher Road, S. W.
Santa Monica, Cal. 90406	Alton, Mo. 63123	Far Rockaway, N. Y. 11691	Atlanta 11, Ga.
213 393 4901	314 ME 1 6049	212 GR 1 0897	404 758 2996

CTION OF MARGARET MITCHELLS

THE WIND"

A frequently used publicity poster, here reproduced on the cover of the Exhibitor's Campaign Book distributed by MGM.

POSTERS and LOBBY CARDS

ORDER ALL ACCESSORIES DIRECTLY FROM NATIONAL SCREEN

6-SHEET

ONE-SHEET

3-SHEET

22 x 28 CARD

WINDOW CARD

INSERT CARD

- —Ask the mayor to proclaim Gone With the Wind's arrival as "the greatest motion picture of all time" and display his proclamation in your lobby.
- —Conduct a search for the nearest lookalike to Vivien Leigh in your community.
- —Pass out Georgia peaches to those in line at the opening performance. Arrange with the local supermarket to send peaches to newspaper critics.
- —Obtain a horse-drawn carriage and dress a couple in Civil War clothes to ride in it.
- —Look for any babies who were christened Rhett or Scarlett and arrange radio interviews with their parents.
- —Run a coloring contest. Have customers pick up drawings at supermarkets, banks and gas stations and color drawings of Scarlett shooting the Yankee, Atlanta in flames, and Rhett carrying Scarlett upstairs.

LOBBY DISPLAYS.

Theatre owners were supplied with five-foot medallions that pictured a smoldering Rhett and Scarlett . . . framed portraits of the four stars . . . a dozen color stills from the movie . . . an assortment of posters and lobby cards ranging from large to immense . . . day-glo displays, self-standing signs, streamers, valances and usher badges.

PRODUCT TIE-INS.

Retailers selling such disparate products as rings, dolls, nylons, flowers, stamps and candy featured Gone With the Wind in their newspaper ads . . . A "Scarlett Nectar Ice Cream Soda" was promoted by a drugstore chain . . . A jewelry firm advertised "The Scarlett," a brooch with simulated pearls alternating with simulated rubies . . . The Greyhound Bus Line promoted the film on buses headed for Atlanta, and Delta Airlines promoted the plane that carried in the film.

CANNED NEWSPAPER STORIES.

Exhibitors were given an assortment of newspaper stories prepared in Culver City and designed to be sent to the entertainment editor of the newspapers in which the theatres advertised. The stories presented the facts of the film from the most newsworthy angles. Typical headlines:

"SOUTHERNERS RECONCILED TO ENGLISH SCARLETT, GLAD SHE WON'T BE PLAYED BY A YANKEE"

"MARGARET MITCHELL ORIGINALLY NAMED HER HEROINE PANSY"

"DIRECTOR FLEMING NEVER READ NOVEL"

"TOOK PERSUASION TO SIGN HOWARD FOR ASHLEY ROLE"

"GABLE WON'T CRY"

FUTURES

All their paths led to Gone With the Wind — *Gable, Leigh, de Havilland, Howard, Selznick, Cukor, Fleming.* But where did their paths lead away from that epic union?

VIVIEN LEIGH: AFTERMATH.

Be careful what you wish for, said the philosopher, for you may get it. Vivien Leigh got the role she wished for,

even won an Academy Award for her portrayal, but she remained bitter over it till the day she died.

In the years following her long stay at Tara, illness plagued Vivien Leigh, both physical and emotional. Tuberculosis laid siege to her body, recurring frequently.

Meanwhile, life went on in the incestuous atmosphere of Hollywood and New York. In 1947, Irene Selznick, now divorced from David Selznick, turned to producing plays on Broadway. She produced a drama called A Streetcar Named Desire, perhaps feeling a certain déjà vu in a story about a Southern belle. The play starred Marlon Brando, Kim Hunter and Jessica Tandy in the role of the vulnerable Blanche DuBois. Warner Bros. bought the screen rights to Streetcar and Jack Warner decided to move the entire Broadway company to Hollywood — with one notable exception. In the role of the Southern belle he cast Vivien Leigh.

Vivien Leigh with Claude Rains in Caesar and Cleopatra *(1945)*

The role of Blanche DuBois was like a grisly homecoming for Vivien. The muses were laughing, for the actress could not escape the mold she had created. In Streetcar Vivien Leigh was playing a Southern belle fighting decline. She knew her role all too well. And for it, she won her second Academy Award.

It seemed impossible for Vivien Leigh to escape the role of the bedeviled woman, a fate she shared with Bette Davis. In The Roman Spring of Mrs. Stone, a film she made with Warren Beatty in 1964, once again she played a neurotic, vulnerable woman.

But whatever the role, Vivien Leigh continued to be driven. Hard on the heels of an exhausting world tour with the Old Vic, she went into rehearsals for a Broadway musical called Tovarich. Vivien rarely left the stage, as she played a Russian countess forced to seek employment as a domestic with an American family. When she danced the Charleston with the young son, there was magic afoot in the Broadway Theatre.

But Vivien was not through playing Southern belles. The gods of Hollywood type-casting are relentless. In 1965, when Columbia Pictures brought Katherine Anne Porter's Ship of Fools to the screen, the all-star cast was headed by Vivien Leigh in the role of a Southern belle. This time it was the

Leigh with Marlon Brando in A Streetcar Named Desire *(1951)*

Leigh with Lee Marvin in Ship of Fools *(1965)*

Clark Gable with Adolphe Menjou in The Hucksters (1947)

Gable in Command Decision (1949)

charismatic Lee Marvin who found himself playing opposite her. Like Gable and Brando before him, he was eclipsed by Vivien's mixture of elegance and fury.

Vivien Leigh was a woman of spirit. Like the John O'Hara heroine, she had a rage to live. Since 1945 she had been ravaged by tuberculosis and in 1967 she suffered another recurrence. This time the frail body could not match the strong will. On July 8, at the age of fifty-four, Vivien Leigh's struggles came to an end.

CLARK GABLE: AFTERMATH.

The Japanese attacked Pearl Harbor on December 7, 1941. Six weeks later a plane that was carrying Carole Lombard on a war-bond selling tour crashed in Nevada with all lives lost.

It was a cruel jest that destiny had played on the King of Hollywood. A scant two years after he had reluctantly undertaken a film that would enable him to marry Carole Lombard, a plane crash had taken her away from him. Gable promptly enlisted in the army and volunteered for overseas duty which took him on many hazardous bombing missions over Germany. He was a tailgunner — some said he was the only commissioned tailgunner in the air force — and was discharged two years later with the rank of major.

Gable returned to Hollywood to do the only work he knew. He was a precious commodity to the studio to which he returned. He was costarred with the new crop of actresses who were being nurtured by MGM during the war years. Chief among these was the saintly Greer Garson. During the war years Miss Garson had brought her martyred trademark to Mrs. Miniver and Random Harvest. How she was united with the returning Gable in a forgettable film called

Adventure, with director Victor Fleming to supply Gable with a comfortable environment.

When Frederic Wakeman's novel about the compromises of advertising men, The Hucksters, hit the best-seller lists, MGM bought the rights as a vehicle for Gable, this time pairing him with Deborah Kerr.

In 1953 Gable left MGM and began working in a freelance fashion that signaled the decline of the Hollywood studios. He had always been bitter over

not sharing in the immense profits of Gone With the Wind. Now, for the first time, he would receive a

percentage of the profits of his films. Unfortunately, this new freedom was not as productive as it was for Olivia de Havilland. In this final phase of his career, Gable made few distinguished films. He appeared with Susan Hayward in Soldier of Fortune and in other equally unimpressive films. Even when he sought to recapture the mystique of the Old South in Band of Angels, the film

Gable with Marilyn Monroe in The Misfits (1961)

was a pale copy of the Selznick original.

In 1960 playwright Arthur Miller wrote a screenplay called The Misfits, and in the three starring roles United Artists cast Clark Gable, Marilyn Monroe and Montgomery Clift. It was a creative marriage of volatile forces. Laboring on location in the hot Nevada sun, Gable was drained by fatigue. The film's climax included a horse-roping sequence. Gable obstinately refused to use a stuntman. Who can say what moved him to such a decision? Perhaps a desire to

show that at fifty-nine he still had the manliness that was the subject of such self-doubt all his life. Whatever the reason, within forty-eight hours after filming ended for the project, Clark Gable was stricken by a heart attack, and twelve days later was dead.

OLIVIA DE HAVILLAND: AFTERMATH.

Jack Warner was prophetic. As he feared, Olivia de Havilland was spoiled by her taste of freedom. On her return to the Warner Bros. lot, fame followed her. Warner tried to appease her with

better roles, but the damage was done. When her contract expired in 1943, Olivia announced that she had no wish to renew it. Warner was furious. If he could not hold her, at least he could delay her flight. During the course of her seven-year contract, Olivia had refused several assignments, and in consequence been suspended without pay for a total of nine months. When her contract ran out and she failed to renew it, the Warners Business Affairs Office notified Olivia that they were tacking the suspended time onto the end of her contract. The doe-eyed damsel decided to fight. The legal struggle cost her over two years of forced unemployment as the case crawled through the California courts and her legal expenses mounted. But at the end of the tunnel, the courts decided in her favor. The jurists agreed that it was intolerable to permit a studio to add suspension time to contract time.

Thus Olivia de Havilland's career began a new era, one which held much greater creative fulfullment. The demure lovely who had fought her way out of Warner Bros. to appear in Gone With the Wind, had now fought her way out again, this time for good.

As an independent performer, she starred in To Each His Own, a moving film

Olivia de Havilland in The Dark Mirror *(1946)*

De Havilland with Leo Genn in The Snake Pit (1948)

De Havilland with Montgomery Clift and Ralph Richardson in The Heiress (1949)

that won her the Academy Award. Darryl Zanuck starred her in the screen version of the bestseller about anguish in a mental hospital, The Snake Pit. And then to climax her career, in 1949 Olivia starred in The Heiress, an adaptation of Henry James' riveting novel Washington Square. It was a superlative role and brought her still another Academy Award.

In 1955 Olivia married editor Pierre Galante and moved to France. She returned to America occasionally for Oscar ceremonies and the inevitable re-releases of Gone With the Wind, where she eventually became the only surviving star.

One other trip to America was especially gratifying. In

1977 she visited the Kennedy Center in Washington and had the satisfaction of hearing the National Film Institute declare Gone With the Wind the greatest film of all time.

LESLIE HOWARD: AFTERMATH.

When George Bernard Shaw was awarded an Oscar for the screenplay to Pygmalion, the playwright said he had never been so insulted in his life. And when Leslie Howard was seemingly the only one associated with Gone With the Wind who failed to receive either an Oscar or a nomination, he greeted the oversight with similar Shavian disdain.

Leslie Howard's interest lay elsewhere. He had ambitions to direct, and after completing his acting chores in Intermezzo, he sailed for home to establish his own filmmaking unit. He directed a sequel to The Scarlet Pimpernel, and then a drama called The First and the Few. Neither had the distinction of most of Howard's screen roles in which he had been directed by others. It was to prove a Hollywood axiom about the inability of first-rate actors to become first-rate directors. There have been exceptions to the rule, as in the case of Orson Welles, but for every such exception there are many more cases that authenticate it.

Leslie Howard's life came to an abrupt end. He was in Portugal on a lecture tour for the British Council — some said it was a secret mission for the British government. He was flying back to England on the same day that Winston Churchill was due to return home from conferences with his military chiefs at Gibraltar. A German intelligence agent observed a short, stocky, cigar-smoking man climbing up the ramp onto a commercial airliner and radioed this information to Berlin. A squadron of German fighter planes was dispatched to hunt down the unarmed airliner. They blasted it out of the sky. Winston Churchill was not aboard the plane. But Leslie Howard was dead at fifty-three.

GEORGE CUKOR: AFTERMATH.

It might have been supposed that the acrimonious parting of Selznick and Cukor on Gone With the Wind would have created a schism between the two. But to his credit, Selznick promptly lobbied his father-in-law into assigning Cukor to direct The Women. Selznick could see the wisdom of putting the "woman's director" on a film consisting entirely of women. It may be recalled that The Women, adapted from the vitriolic comedy by Clare Boothe, did not have a single man in its cast. What it did have was a collection of actresses who had been considered and rejected for

George Cukor

the role of Scarlett O'Hara.
What more fitting than to have
as their director the man
who was himself a Gone With
the Wind reject. Cukor had
gone from a film about one
bitchy woman to a film about
a bevy of them.

Cukor reunited with
another Scarlett castoff in the
screen adaptation of Philip
Barry's The Philadelphia
Story. Katharine Hepburn's
career was at low ebb
when she took the role of the
socialite on the eve of her
second marriage, and it lifted
her back to the summit.

Four decades after Gone
With the Wind, George
Cukor remains active and
productive. Most recently he
was responsible for the
resonance of a screen version
of Graham Greene's Travels
With My Aunt, in which
Maggie Smith gave a hilarious
performance as a bizarre old
lady who turns her sedate
nephew into a reckless copy
of herself. As in the years
when he molded the
characters of Garbo,
Hepburn, Tallulah and Leigh,
George Cukor was still working his magic with women.

VICTOR FLEMING:
AFTERMATH.

Like many others who were
swept up in the spectacle and
trauma of Gone With the
Wind, Victor Fleming's career
peaked with that production
and never approached the
pinnacle again. His future
work was unimpressive and
his assignments rare.

When Gable returned from
war, Fleming was chosen to
direct his first film on the
theory that he could provide
the returning King with the
support he needed. But the
result was uneven by the
most charitable standards.

The Hemingway stamp was
fading by the time Victor
Fleming directed Spencer
Tracy in A Guy Named Joe
and in Dr. Jekyll and Mr.
Hyde. He next undertook a
portentous version of Joan of
Arc with Ingrid Bergman, and
with that the career of Victor
Fleming slid into limbo.

Like some of the other
principals of GWTW, Fleming
seems to have had a self-
destructive urge. It drove
him to demand a total rewrite
of the script he had been
chosen to direct. It drove him
to curse his female star and
walk off the set, inviting his
own replacement. It drove
him to depreciate a movie
that has become a legend.
And it drove him to poison his
relationship with the producer
who had placed him at the
helm of his greatest
achievement. When Gone
With the Wind was
completed, Selznick wanted
to indicate the contribution of
such people as George
Cukor, William Cameron
Menzies, and Kay Brown
(who first brought the novel
to his attention). He proposed
a separate card in the main
titles that would acknowledge
their contribution. Fleming
loudly objected to such a card
and it was omitted. But the

omission was bought at
the expense of Selznick's
regard, and the two men
never worked together again.
Selznick brought no other
"white elephants" to Victor
Fleming.

SAM WOOD:
AFTERMATH.

The future years were
productive for Sam Wood.
Lacking any real visual sense,
he had the good fortune to
work again with William
Cameron Menzies, the
brilliant production designer
who was the architect of the
visual splendor in Gone With
the Wind.

Menzies was at Sam
Wood's right hand when he
directed For Whom the Bell
Tolls and King's Row, and the
visual excitement of those
films brought a fresh luster to
Wood's career.

In the late forties, Sam
Wood was caught up in the
frenzy of the McCarthy era.
He was as determined to wipe
out Communists in
Hollywood as Scarlett was
determined to wipe out
Yankees in Georgia. He led a
group called the Motion
Picture Alliance for the
Preservation of American
Ideals. He died in 1949 at the
age of sixty-five.

DAVID O. SELZNICK:
AFTERMATH.

The phantom of Gone With
the Wind stunted Selznick's
creative growth. It forced him
to measure every project by a
yardstick that could only
throttle ambition and hobble

hope. For Selznick the inevitable question was, "Will this be better than Gone With the Wind?" The producer seemed to need the reassurance of another resounding success, and a success of this magnitude eluded him.

In the years that followed GWTW, Selznick made few films, and in order to keep his independent company from drowning in red ink, he would loan his collection of contract players — including Gregory Peck, Joan Fontaine and Ingrid Bergman — to the major studios.

He had the story judgment to purchase the rights to several promising novels —

including The Keys of the Kingdom and Waterloo Bridge — then resold them to other producers who were not hobbled by the past.

Eventually David Selznick turned back to filmmaking. But when he did, his motive was associated more with the heart than with the head. Kay Brown who had sent him the novel that obsessed him, now sent him a young actress who produced a similar effect. Her name was Phyllis Isley, and Selznick, with his propensity for improving everything he touched, changed it to Jennifer Jones. He set out to find a film in which to star her. Meanwhile, he brought her together with director

Henry King, who promptly cast her in The Song of Bernadette. Her career was well launched. Selznick finally discovered the ideal vehicle for Jennifer Jones, a six-handkerchief novel called Since You Went Away, which told the story of a home-front family in the midst of World War II. Selznick himself adapted the book to the screen. This time he would not place a middleman between himself and the script. He delivered a hand-picked, star-studded cast that included Claudette Colbert, Shirley Temple, Lionel Barrymore and Hattie McDaniel. Also in the cast was the actress's husband, an ingenuous young man named Robert Walker. As filming progressed, Selznick's ardor for the young woman became more apparent, and it was a stressful time for Phyllis Isley's husband and David Selznick's wife. The film was a success, but the saga of a Northern family in the midst of war could not compare with the saga of a Southern family in the midst of an earlier war. The ghost of Gone With the Wind continued to resist exorcism.

Selznick's appetite for filmmaking seemed to have been energized by the effects of his new love. He next produced Spellbound, a vehicle for two of his major discoveries, Ingrid Bergman and Gregory Peck, and directed by Alfred Hitchcock.

David O. Selznick's Portrait of Jennie (1948), starring Jennifer Jones and Joseph Cotten

Selznick's A Farewell to Arms *(1957)*

Selznick's Notorious *(1946), starring Claude Rains and Ingrid Bergman*

To any other producer Spellbound would have been a most satisfying production; to Selznick it was a disappointment. It was in no way comparable to his legendary epic.

But once more legend beckoned. Niven Busch had written a seething novel called Duel in the Sun. Selznick was seized by the implications of a Western of epic proportions, sort of a sagebrush Gone With the Wind. Once more his star would be Jennifer Jones. In the midst of production, Selznick was abandoned by both his wife and his director. Irene Selznick could no longer adjust to her husband's attachment to his star. And director King Vidor could no longer adjust to his producer's excessive interference.

In all his future productions, David Selznick sought to revive the image of Gone With the Wind, but like a man trying to resume a dream, he found himself clutching at air. The more eagerly he tried to revive the legend, the more it eluded him.

In 1957 Selznick made a last effort to lay to rest the ghost of Scarlett O'Hara. With Jennifer Jones as his star and a script by the redoubtable Ben Hecht, he began production of Hemingway's A Farewell to Arms. Unfortunately, in the starring role Rock Hudson lacked the necessary intensity, and director John Huston refused to bow to Selznick's edicts. An era had arrived where no top-flight director would bow to his producer's pronouncements. Charles Vidor replaced Huston and tried manfully to function despite the shower of memos and telegrams. A Farewell to Arms was the enclosing bookend for Selznick's filmmaking career. A few years later he tried to assemble a musical version of Gone With the Wind for Broadway, but found that you can't go home again. The show never reached the stage in his lifetime. In his final years, Selznick preferred to become an industry monument, a gray eminence who was famous for his past glories and joyous parties.

In 1965 the dynamic heart finally stopped. And all across

Joseph Cotten and Jennifer Jones in Selznick's Duel in the Sun *(1946)*

the country, the obituaries began as he knew they would, with the words, "David O. Selznick, the man who produced Gone With the Wind, died today . . ."

THE CURSE OF *GONE WITH THE WIND.*

The man who wrote the screenplay was crushed by a runaway tractor on his Pennsylvania farm.

The man who played Ashley Wilkes was shot down in an unarmed airliner.

The man who played one of the Tarleton twins and the woman who played the Atlanta madam both took their own lives.

The woman who wrote the original novel was killed by a drunken driver while crossing the street she immortalized.

Olivia de Havilland and Ona Munson

The ghost of Gone With the Wind *haunted many of its creators, as a pinnacle they would never again achieve or with a highly visible exposure that would typecast them unmercifully.*

Notice of Margaret Mitchell's death.

Disaster on Peachtree St.: Margaret Mitchell (inset), 43-year-old author of *Gone With the Wind,* was critically injured when a drunken driver hit her as she walked with her husband on Peachtree St., Atlanta, Ga. The famous street figures prominently in her novel of Civil War years and in the film. Here Scarlett O'Hara (Vivien Leigh) avoids a plunging horse as she gets news during Atlanta siege.

MARGARET MITCHELL.

She was critically injured when a drunken driver struck her as she and her husband crossed Atlanta's Peachtree Street, which figured so prominently in her novel. She was forty-nine.

SIDNEY HOWARD.

The famous playwright was in a barn on his Pennsylvania farm, turning the crank on his tractor to start the engine. Unknown to Howard, the vehicle was in gear and when the engine engaged, the tractor lurched forward, crushing him to death against the wall. He was forty-eight.

ONA MUNSON.

She felt that Gone With the Wind *had forever typecast her as the madam with a heart of gold. She received only similar roles in the future. Suffering from depression, she took her own*

173

life with an overdose of sleeping pills. She was forty-nine.

F. SCOTT FITZGERALD.

Fired from Gone With the Wind *on the very eve of production, beset by bills and doubts, the novelist's self-confidence was dealt a lethal blow. Fitzgerald*

F. Scott Fitzgerald

Tribute to Leslie Howard in Photoplay *magazine.*

We Won't Forget

plunged into a cycle of drink and depression. He died eighteen months later. He was forty-four.

LESLIE HOWARD.

He journeyed to Portugal on a lecture tour for the British government. The Germans believed that his plane carried Prime Minister Winston Churchill. The airliner was blasted out of the sky, killing everyone aboard. Leslie Howard was fifty-three.

GEORGE REEVES.

The actor who played one of the Tarleton twins enjoyed great success as Superman in the famous TV series, but he later grew depressed that his career had been demolished by his association with the comic book character. He died at his own hand of a gunshot wound. He was forty-five.

CAROLE LOMBARD.

On a war-bond tour, Mrs. Clark Gable was aboard a plane that crashed in the Nevada mountains near Las Vegas. She was killed instantly. She was thirty-six.

LAURA HOPE CREWS.

Two years after GWTW premiered with Miss Crews in the role of Aunt Pittypat, she was striken with a kidney disease while starring on Broadway in Arsenic and Old Lace. *She died at sixty-two.*

WARD BOND.

He played the Yankee captain in the Raid on Shanty Town Scene. Bond had finally reached genuine fame on TV's "Wagon Train" series when he died suddenly of a heart attack. He was fifty-seven.

LOUIS B. MAYER.

He died in 1957, stripped of his power at Hollywood's largest studio. His stars were going independent. Television was undermining the moviegoing habit. Mayer was dead and the studio system was dying.

George Reeves

Carole Lombard

THE LASTING IMPACT OF GONE WITH THE WIND

**COUNTESS ISSERLYN MAKEUP.
IT WAS CREATED FOR THE WOMEN
EVERY OTHER WOMAN WANTED TO LOOK LIKE.**

There was something electric about the great stars then.
The way they looked, dressed, walked and even talked was alluring and exciting.
And the makeup they wore was part of their magic. For it illuminated their complexions
and made everything about them look radiant. That makeup was Countess Isserlyn.
Countess Isserlyn makeup is as radiant as it ever was. It's the classic of all makeups today.
And the women who wear it are often like the stars. The envy of every woman.
COUNTESS ISSERLYN MAKEUP BY ALEXANDRA DE MARKOFF
Available in liquid or creme

Until television arrived to provide a late-night resting place for the films of yesteryear, a motion picture had a life of about two weeks. After that period, when a film had saturated the neighborhood theatres, it passed into oblivion. Gone With the Wind was something else entirely. It was designed for the ages and it was to become a part of our culture.

The film itself and all its major stars have crept into our consciousness and continue to wink at us from the most improbable places.

The cat eyes of Vivien Leigh stare out at us from a magazine ad for Countess Isserlyn Makeup.

Rhett Butler lives on in a gossipy page of "Frankly, My Dear, I Don't Give a Damn Awards."

Margaret Mitchell remains alive in the blurbs of booksellers, when her name is invoked by a book reviewer in praise of a new romantic novel.

In New York magazine we

learn that on the list of the most demanded books in the libraries of New York, Gone With the Wind *leads all the other millions of volumes.*

Across the continent, in the Los Angeles Times, the Pickwick Bookstores advertise a book called Scarlett Fever, *coupling it with the paperback version of an earlier one called* Scarlett, Rhett and a Cast of Thousands.

Meanwhile, the readers of Daily Variety *examine an ad which Gavin Lambert, author of still another book another book on* Gone With the Wind, *is announced as the screenwriter of the motion picture adaption of the bestselling biography of Vivien Leigh by Anne Edwards, who is hard at work on the screenplay for the sequel to* Gone With the Wind.

While newspapers around the country breathlessly report that Gone With the Wind, *Hollywood's most celebrated film, has established still another milestone in its continuing legend by bringing MGM no less than thirty-five million dollars from CBS for a twenty-year television run.*

And so the impact of Gone With the Wind *goes on.*

From 1939 to 1980 seems but the wink of an eye to this evergreen colossus which continues to leap at us from unexpected quarters, proving what we knew all along, that life begins at forty.

RHETT BUTLER'S "FRANKLY, MY DEAR, I DON'T GIVE A DAMN!" AWARD

SCARLETT: But, Rhett, where will I go, what will become of me?

RHETT: Frankly, my dear, I don't give a damn!

What utter contempt and rejection Clark Gable, in Gone With The Wind, expressed toward Vivian Leigh with these famous words! They're also a perfect expression of our sentiments toward certain hot stories which, somehow, leave us cold. Here, then, are the ten items which have won themselves the securest places in this issue's Frankly-My-Dear-I-Don't-Give-A-Damn Department!

1. Lynda Bird's wedding to What's-His-Name.

2. George Hamilton's cracking good-sportsmanship about same.

3. Pat Morrow's marathon romance with Chris Connelly.

4. Marlo Thomas's ditto with Len Goldberg.

5. Tina Sinatra's ditto ditto with Sammy Hess.

6. Princess Lee Radziwell's sudden soar to stardom without even a bit of help, honey!

7. Barbara Parkins' constant commuting to Rome in the search of (Hah!) romance.

8. Sally Fields' weekend whirl in New York with Davy Jones (a put-up job if ever

9. Everybody's sudden, fervent longing to join The Beatles in meditating with Maharish Yogi. ("Who's your little guru, Who's your turtle dove...?)

THE Hollywood REPORTER

Vol. CCLI, No. 3   Hollywood, California, Thursday, April 6, 1978   Price 35 Cents

Media ownership may be subject of FTC hearing
From The Hollywood Reporter
Washington Bureau

WASHINGTON — The FTC has begun "a very initial inquiry" into "the problems of media concentration," according to Daniel Schwartz, deputy director of the FTC's bureau of competition.

Schwartz told The Hollywood Reporter: "Basically, we're considering whether or not a problem exists with regard to joint ownership of a range of different sources of media outlets — newspaper/TV, different book publishing and other outlets. . . ." He stressed that this is an initial project, and that no formal investigation is under way at this time.

The FTC has begun its inquiry by requesting an economic study done by the FCC six years ago on media conglomerates, defined by an FCC staff member as multiindustry companies that indicated broadcasting among the sphere of their activities.

The FCC is "evaluating" at this time whether to turn the report over to the FTC, since it contains certain unpublished internal financial records "theoretically given in a confidential manner" to the FCC, said an FCC source.

Cates Brothers slate 'Accursed' for late '78 start
By HEDY KLEYWEG

The Cates Brothers Co. has finalized negotiations for a feature property marked for a 1978 production start in addition to its two-picture deal with NBC and three primetime TV specials set for May. Gil Cates, who also works independent of the company partner Joseph, is preparing to direct a film for 20th Century-Fox and has just completed a feature for Universal.

Recently firmed were the rights to "Accursed," a horror story written by
— continued on page 21

'Gone With the Wind(fall)' for MGM; CBS pays $35 million
By KEVIN McDONALD

"Gone With the Wind," Hollywood's most celebrated film, has set yet another milestone by fetching $35 million from CBS for a 20-year run in the biggest licensing deal ever for a feature film. It will bow on the network next season, according to CBS Entertainment president Robert A. Daly.

The sale provides an immediate windfall to MGM, the picture's owner, which will receive payment in equal installments over the next five years, and record the revenue over four years. That works out to around $8.75 million per reporting year, and will first show up in the current fiscal year's fourth quarter, which ends August 31.

Since David O. Selznick's 1939 production has long since been paid off, nearly all of the $8.75 million will filter down into the pretax profit category. That's equal to about 17% of the company's entire pretax profit for all of its last fiscal year.

The development wasn't lost on Wall Street, which quickly pushed up the price of MGM's common stock
— continued on page 4

New Ventures green-lights first group of 7 projects
By ROGER CELS

MCA New Ventures, having waded through over 3,500 applicants for funding during its year and a half in existence, has given the green light to its first wave of projects, with several scheduled to get under way over the next few months, president Norbert Simmons disclosed.

Three stage plays, a film project, a record company, an educational film production company and a catering concern have received the go-ahead, representing a cash investment by New Ventures of somewhere between $2.5 million and $4 million, depending on the outcome of specific negotiations.

One of the plays, Neil Simon's "Gingerbread Lady," is scheduled to open within the next two weeks at the Ebony Showcase Theatre in Los
— continued on page 4

Hollywood General into production with comedy 'Hurt'
By FRANK BARRON

Hollywood General Studios, starting its third year, is moving into production itself, and will be involved with producer Pat Curtis and authorcomic Larry Wilde on coproduction of a comedy film called "It Couldn't Hurt," based on various jokes from Wilde's numerous ethnic joke books.

A tie-in will be made with Pinnacle Books, which publishes the Wilde humor, to promote the film, which is slated to be a Christmas release as an R-rated movie.

HGS president Glen Speidel and vp Lloyd Gaynes will be executive producers, with Curtis' Curtco Prods. the line producers. Gaynes called it "a sort of 'Tunnelvision' and 'Kentucky Fried Movie,' at a low budget. We'll use college students in the vignettes,
— continued on page 21

Jet artists vow to resist move from UA Records
By DIANNE BENNETT

Don Arden, president of Jet Records and manager of Jet recording artist Electric Light Orchestra, has stated emphatically that under no circumstances will Jet or any of its artists be a part of the rumored sale of United Artists Records to an EMIfunded group headed by current UA Records president Artie Mogull and ex-ABC Records president Jerry Rubinstein. Negotiating price is said to be in the neighborhood of $40 million.

Worldwide sales of ELO and other
— continued on page 4

New World turns to foreign markets for more revenue
By JEFF FREEDMAN

New World Pictures, often linked with exploitation films which fill the drive-in circuit domestically, plans to focus more heavily on the international market as a source of revenue for its product, according to Ed Carlin, director of international sales and distribution for the company.

The first implementation of this policy will see New World giving "I Never Promised You a Rose Garden" one of the biggest openings of any film in Paris. On May 26 the film will bow in 40 theatres. To promote the film, New World has allocated $250,000 in advertising.

By comparison, the company's
— continued on page 21

THE *GONE WITH THE WIND* NOSTALGIA QUIZ

1. When Scarlett goes to visit Rhett who is in a Yankee prison, her purpose is to (   ). Her gown is made from Tara's (   ). She plays the affluent lady but is given away by her (   ).

2. The blonde girl gossiping at the Twelve Oaks reception is actress (   ) who years later co-starred with (   ) in (   ) in which he sang her the Irving Berlin classic (   ).

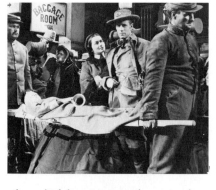

4. Ashley is on a (   ) furlough from the front. (   ) and (   ) meet him at the (   ) amidst a flood of Confederate casualties.

3. Blockade-runner Rhett brings a hat to Scarlett from (   ) in the midst of her mourning over the death of her first husband (   ).

5. (   ) declares her love to (   ) whose engagement to (   ) has just been announced, unaware that (   ) is listening on the sofa.

6. (   ) argues with Rhett about the ease with which the South would win the impending war. Rhett feels the North's advantage lies in its (   ) and the South's lack of everything but (   ).

7. (   ) had declared extensive experience in (   ) but faced with the task, she admits that she lied. In a fury, Scarlett (   ).

8. Scarlett searches for (   ) among the wounded at the (   ). She needs him to (   ).

9. (   ) and (   ) played Scarlett's two sisters. The former had only one previous film credit, The Buccaneer in 1938, and the latter had done only two films, both of them with Mickey Rooney in tales of the (   ) family.

10. In the famous Paddock Scene, Scarlett pleads with Ashley to (   ), but he is dissuaded by (   ). This was the scene from Vivien's screen test in which she was directed by (   ).

11. Ashley has been wounded in a raid on (   ), where earlier in the day

(   ) had been saved from assault by the intervention of her former foreman, (   ).

12. Scarlett scandalizes (   ) by appearing in her widow's weeds at the dance at the (   ), and waltzing with gunrunner (   ). (   ) promptly calls for her smelling salts.

13. Scarlett is pressed into service by (   ), played by (   ), as the troops of (   ) sweep toward Atlanta.

14. Scarlett's second husband, ( ), was played by ( ). She stole him from her younger sister, ( ), played by ( ).

15. The quintessential Southern Mammy was played by ( ). She argues with Scarlett over ( ) to the barbecue at ( ).

16. War has broken out and ( ) prepares to leave for the front, leaving behind him the women who love him, his

gentle wife ( ) and the tempestuous ( ).

17. Rhett gave Scarlett a frenzied buggyride through the riot-ridden streets of ( ). Their destination was the home of ( ) who was preparing her own flight from the city.

18. Scarlett wears black in unfelt bereavement over the battlefield death of her first husband ( ), played by ( ). The young lieutenant had died not of wounds but of ( ).

NOSTALGIA QUIZ ANSWERS.

1. Borrow money/drapes/ hands
2. Marjorie Reynolds/Bing Crosby/Holiday Inn/White Christmas
3. Paris/Charles Hamilton
4. Two weeks/Melanie/ Scarlett/Atlanta Terminal
5. Scarlett/Ashley/Melanie/ Rhett
6. Charles Hamilton/ factories and fleet/arrogance
7. Prissy/birthing babies/ slaps her face
8. Dr. Meade/Atlanta depot/deliver Melanie's baby
9. Evelyn Keyes/Ann Rutherford/Hardy
10. Run away with her/ honor/George Cukor
11. Shantytown/Scarlett/ Big Sam
12. Atlanta society/armory/ Rhett Butler/Aunt Pittypat
13. Dr. Meade/Harry Davenport/General Sherman
14. Frank Kennedy/Carroll Nye/Suellen O'Hara/Evelyn Keyes
15. Hattie McDaniel/which gown to wear/Twelve Oaks
16. Ashley/Melanie/Scarlett
17. Atlanta/Pittypat
18. Charles Hamilton/Rand Brooks/measles

449,512   feet of color film were shot totaling 88 hours.

160,000   feet of film were printed

20,300   feet of edited film totaling 3 hours 45 minutes.

1,500   sketches of sets were drawn.

200   sets were designed.

90   sets were constructed.

3,000   sketches of shot setups were made covering every scene in the film.

53   buildings were erected to re-create the city of Atlanta.

7,000   feet of streets were laid for the city of Atlanta.

3,000   feet of the reconstructed Peachtree Street were laid.

1,000,000   feet of lumber were used to build the sets.

1,100   horses were used.

375   other animals were used, including dogs, mules, oxen, cows and pigs.

450   vehicles were used, including wagons, gun-caissons and ambulances.

59   members of the cast.

12,000   days of employment in shooting schedule.

2,400   extras and bit players.

1,350,000	*feet of film ran through the cameras.*
10,000	*antiques were offered for sale in the Charity Bazaar Scene.*
25	*cameos were purchased in the U.S. and Europe for Scarlett's dresses.*
7	*Technicolor cameras filmed the Atlanta fire with flames leaping 500 feet from a set that covered 40 acres.*
10	*pieces of fire equipment from the Los Angeles Fire Department, 25 policemen, 50 studio firemen and 200 studio helpers controlled the Atlanta fire.*
15,000	*gallons of water doused the Atlanta fire after filming.*
1,000,000	*feet of film would have been required to film the entire novel and the resulting film would have taken one week to show.*
250,000	*man hours were spent in pre-production before a foot of film was shot.*
750,000	*man hours were spent in actual production.*
2,500	*costumes were worn by the female characters.*
7	*bales of cotton went into the female wardrobe.*
$10,000	*cleaning bill for wardrobe during production.*
34	*different carpet designs were created for the film.*
36	*wallpaper designs were hand-painted.*
12	*days the shooting was closed down when George Cukor was dismissed.*
$30,000	*Vivien Leigh's salary.*
$10,000	*total salary of supporting characters from Hattie McDaniel on down.*
$446,688	*stars and supporting payroll.*
$108,469	*extras payroll.*
$1,408,997	*technicians payroll.*
550	*separate items of wardrobe were created.*
377	*costume sketches made by Walter Plunkett.*
44	*costume sketches for Rhett.*

21	costume changes for Melanie.
11	costume changes for Ashley.
$153,818	cost of costumes.
$2,500,000	projected production cost of which half was contributed by MGM, the rest by Selznick backers.
$3,700,000	actual production cost.
$3,957,000	final cost including overhead for prints, advertising, publicity and distribution.
469	feature films released in 1939.
125	shooting days for Vivien Leigh.
71	shooting days for Clark Gable.
59	shooting days for Olivia de Havilland.
32	shooting days for Leslie Howard.
21	weeks for principal photography.
23	weeks for editing.
10,000	copies of novel initially printed.
176,000	copies sold within three weeks.
1,000,000	copies sold within six months.
1,690,000	copies sold within one year.
1,037	pages to the novel.
500,000	words to the novel.
3½ lbs.	the novel's weight.
$3	price of the novel, $2.75 pre-publication price.
864	pages to paperback edition, largest ever published.
2,500	extras ordered for Confederate Wounded Scene.
1,500	extras supplied by Screen Extras Guild.

1,000	dummies used to augment live extras.
$197,877	cost to build sets.
$35,000	cost of lumber and materials.
$153,818	wardrobe cost.
$109,974	cost of Technicolor film stock.
$5,511	cost of soundtrack stock.
$10,363	cost of developing and printing soundtrack.
$134,497	lighting cost.
$59,917	cost of transportation.
$96,758	rental and purchase of props.
$54,341	location fees.
$40,000,000	estimated cost of remaking GWTW 20 years later.
75¢	tickets to morning and afternoon performances.
$1	tickets to evening performances.
$1.50	reserved seats for evening performances.
70%	MGM's share of the gross box-office receipts from theatre owners.
25,000,000	people had seen GWTW by the end of 1940.
$14,000,000	grossed at box office in one year.
8,100	theatres showed GWTW in general release after a year of road shows.
24,000,000	additional people saw GWTW in its general release.
10,500,000	additional people saw GWTW in its third time around.
$945,000	grossed by film in first week.
$32,000,000	grossed domestically by July 1943.

1,400	*candidates interviewed in search for Scarlett.*
90	*candidates given screen tests.*
$92,000	*cost of screen-testing possible Scarletts.*
142,000	*feet of black-and-white film used in Scarlett tests.*
13,000	*feet of Technicolor film used in Scarlett tests.*
2,500	*seats in Atlanta's Grand Theatre for premiere.*
150,000	*people who greeted motorcade of stars from Atlanta airport.*
$10	*price of tickets to Atlanta premiere.*
5,200	*attended gala charity ball in Atlanta.*
13	*Oscar nominations.*
10	*Oscars won.*
$75,000,000	*domestic and Canadian gross.*
$50,000	*purchase price of motion picture rights to novel.*
$50,000	*voluntarily sent to Miss Mitchell after film released.*
.0007%	*of the movie's gross represented by cost of rights.*
600,000	*viewers saw GWTW in East Berlin in the 1950s where it ran for two and a half years.*
8,000,000	*copies of GWTW were sold throughout the world by 1956.*
25	*countries have had editions of GWTW published in 28 languages.*
100,000,000	*people had seen the film somewhere in the world by 1956.*
$33,500,000	*total rentals of GWTW by 1960 per* Variety *list of all-time box-office grossers.*
$7,700,000	*rentals from 1961 reisue of GWTW.*
$41,200,000	*total rentals of GWTW in 1961.*
$35,000,000	*paid by CBS for 20-year television run.*

1947

GONE WITH THE WIND

GONE WITH
THE WIND

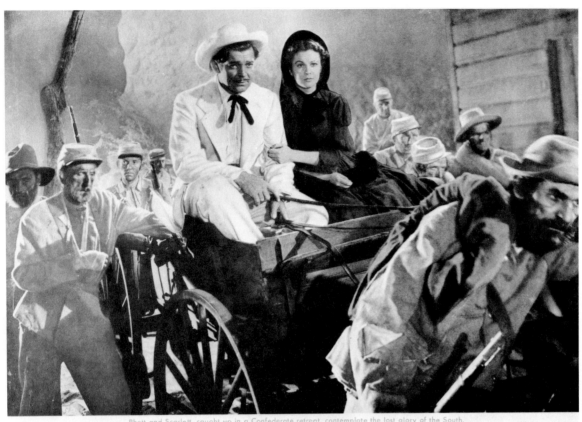

Rhett and Scarlett, caught up in a Confederate retreat, contemplate the lost glory of the South.

David O. Selznick's production in Technicolor® **"GONE WITH THE WIND"** A Metro-Goldwyn-Mayer Release

Atlanta is in Panic; Scarlett races frantically through the crowded streets.

David O. Selznick's production in Technicolor® **"GONE WITH THE WIND"** A Metro-Goldwyn-Mayer Release

Honeymooning in New Orleans, Rhett and Scarlett enjoy the happiness of their marriage.

DAVID O. SELZNICK'S
production of
MARGARET MITCHELL'S **"GONE WITH THE WIND"**

Barred from his wife's room, Rhett Butler finds understanding and consolation from Ona Munson.

"GONE WITH THE WIND"

189

BIBLIOGRAPHY

BOOKS

Felix Barker. The Oliviers. *Lippincott, 1953.*

Rudy Behlmer (editor). Memo from David O. Selznick. *Viking Press, 1972.*

Bosley Crowther. Hollywood Rajah. *Holt, Rinehart and Winston, 1960.*

Bosley Crowther. The Lion's Share. *E. P. Dutton, 1957.*

Alan Dent. Vivien Leigh. *Hamish Hamilton, London, 1972.*

Howard Dietz. Dancing in the Dark. *Quadrangle, 1974.*

Anne Edwards. Vivien Leigh. *Simon and Schuster, 1977.*

Gabe Essoe. The Films of Clark Gable. *Citadel Press, 1970.*

Finish Farr. Margaret Mitchell of Atlanta. *William Morrow, 1957.*

Roland Flamini. Scarlett, Rhett, and a Cast of Thousands. *Macmillan, 1975.*

Gene Fowler. Myron Selznick. *Charlemagne Press, 1944.*

Ezra Goodman. The Fifty Year Decline and Fall of Hollywood. *Simon and Schuster, 1961.*

Sheila Graham and Gerold Frank. Beloved Infidel. *Henry Holt, 1951.*

Richard Griffith. The Movie Stars. *Doubleday, 1970.*

Warren G. Harris. Gable and Lombard. *Simon and Schuster, 1974.*

Richard Harwell (editor). Margaret Mitchell's Gone With the Wind Letters 1936-1949. *Macmillan, 1976.*

Ben Hecht. A Child of the Century. *Simon and Schuster, 1954.*

Leslie Ruth Howard. A Quite Remarkable Father. *Harcourt, Brace and Co., 1959.*

Karol Kulik, Alexander Korda: the Man Who Could Work Miracles. *Arlington House, 1975.*

Gavin Lambert, GWTW. *Atlantic-Little, Brown, 1973.*

_____. On Cukor. *G. P. Putnam's Sons, 1972.*

Aaron Latham. Crazy Sundays. *Viking Press, 1971.*

Samuel Marx. Mayer and Thalberg. *Random House, 1975.*

Margaret Mitchell. Gone With the Wind. *Macmillan, 1936.*

Peter Noble. The Negro in Films. *Arno Press, 1970.*

Hortense Powdermaker. Hollywood: The Dream Factory. *Little, Brown, 1950.*

William Pratt. Scarlett Fever. *Macmillan, 1977.*

David Ragan. Who's Who in Hollywood 1900-1976. *Arlington House, 1976.*

Leo Rosten. Hollywood: The Movie Colony, The Movie Makers. *Harcourt, Brace, 1941.*

William L. Shirer. The Rise and Fall of the Third Reich. *Simon and Schuster, 1960.*

Bob Thomas. Selznick. *Doubleday, 1970.*

_____. Thalberg: Life and Legend. *Doubleday, 1970.*

Lyn Tornabene. Long Live the King: The Biography of Clark Gable. *G. P. Putnam's Sons, 1976.*

Andrew Turnbull (editor). The Letters of F. Scott Fitzgerald. *Dell, 1966.*

Norman Zierold. The Moguls. *Coward McCann, 1969.*

NEWSPAPERS AND MAGAZINES

Atlanta Constitution
Daily Variety
Films in Review
Hollywood Magazine
Hollywood Reporter
Los Angeles Examiner
Los Angeles Magazine
Los Angeles Times
Modern Screen
Movie Mirror
Newsweek
New York Daily News
New Yorker
New York Magazine
New York Times
Photoplay
Pictorial Review
Publisher's Weekly
Reader's Digest
Screen Guide
Screenland
Screen Romances
Silver Screen
Time
Women's Wear Daily

INDEX